Connect

1

Jack C. Richards
Carlos Barbisan
with Chuck Sandy

CAMBRIDGE
UNIVERSITY PRESS

PUBLISHED BY THE PRESS SYNDICATE OF THE UNIVERSITY OF CAMBRIDGE
The Pitt Building, Trumpington Street, Cambridge, United Kingdom

CAMBRIDGE UNIVERSITY PRESS
The Edinburgh Building, Cambridge CB2 2RU, UK
40 West 20th Street, New York, NY 10011–4211, USA
477 Williamstown Road, Port Melbourne, VIC 3207, Australia
Ruiz de Alarcón 13, 28014 Madrid, Spain
Dock House, The Waterfront, Cape Town 8001, South Africa

http://www.cambridge.org

First published 2004
2nd printing 2004

Printed in Hong Kong, China

Typeface New Century Schoolbook   *System* QuarkXPress®

ISBN 0 521 59498 7 Student's Book 1 (English)
ISBN 0 521 60074 X Student's Book 1 (Portuguese)
ISBN 0 521 59495 2 Workbook 1 (English)
ISBN 0 521 60070 7 Workbook 1 (Portuguese)
ISBN 0 521 59494 4 Teacher's Edition 1 (English)
ISBN 0 521 59492 8 Teacher's Edition 1 (Portuguese)
ISBN 0 521 59491 X Class Audio Cassettes 1
ISBN 0 521 59488 X Class CD 1
ISBN 0 521 59487 1 Student's Book 2 (English)
ISBN 0 521 60073 1 Student's Book 2 (Portuguese)
ISBN 0 521 59484 7 Workbook 2 (English)
ISBN 0 521 60069 3 Workbook 2 (Portuguese)
ISBN 0 521 59493 6 Teacher's Edition 2 (English)
ISBN 0 521 59481 2 Teacher's Edition 2 (Portuguese)
ISBN 0 521 59480 4 Class Audio Cassettes 2
ISBN 0 521 59477 4 Class CD 2

ISBN 0 521 59476 6 Student's Book 3 (English)
ISBN 0 521 60072 3 Student's Book 3 (Portuguese)
ISBN 0 521 59475 8 Workbook 3 (English)
ISBN 0 521 60068 5 Workbook 3 (Portuguese)
ISBN 0 521 59483 9 Teacher's Edition 3 (English)
ISBN 0 521 59474 X Teacher's Edition 3 (Portuguese)
ISBN 0 521 59473 1 Class Audio Cassettes 3
ISBN 0 521 59471 5 Class CD 3
ISBN 0 521 59470 7 Student's Book 4 (English)
ISBN 0 521 60071 5 Student's Book 4 (Portuguese)
ISBN 0 521 59469 3 Workbook 4 (English)
ISBN 0 521 60064 2 Workbook 4 (Portuguese)
ISBN 0 521 59482 0 Teacher's Edition 4 (English)
ISBN 0 521 59468 5 Teacher's Edition 4 (Portuguese)
ISBN 0 521 59467 7 Class Audio Cassettes 4
ISBN 0 521 59464 2 Class CD 4

Book design, art direction, and layout services: Adventure House, NYC

Table of Contents

SYLLABUS

Unit 1 – Back to School

Lesson	Function	Grammar	Vocabulary	Theme Project
Lesson 1 Classmates	Introducing yourself	*What's your name?*	Ways to say hello	Make a poster about a classmate.
Lesson 2 Hello.	Greeting someone	*How are you?*	Greetings	
Lesson 3 After school	Introducing others	*this is* (name)	Ways to say good-bye	
Lesson 4 Names	Spelling names	Names	Common American names	
Lesson 5 Connections	Reading • Listening Writing			

Unit 2 – Favorite People

Lesson	Function	Grammar	Vocabulary	Theme Project
Lesson 6 Teachers and friends	Talking about teachers and friends	*his / her* *Who's this?*	Teachers and classmates	Make a poster about a person who works at your school.
Lesson 7 Favorite stars	Talking about favorite stars	*He's / She's . . .*	Stars and their jobs	
Lesson 8 Birthday party	Talking about age	*How old . . . ?* *He's not / She's not*	Numbers 0–20	
Lesson 9 E-pals	Talking about where someone is from	*Where . . . from?* *You're / I'm not*	Countries	
Lesson 10 Connections	Reading • Listening Writing			

Unit 3 – Everyday Things

Lesson	Function	Grammar	Vocabulary	Theme Project
Lesson 11 What a mess!	Describing who owns specific things	*This is / That's +* possessive	Things students own	Make a poster for a department store.
Lesson 12 Cool things	Talking about interesting things	*What's this / that?*	Interesting objects	
Lesson 13 Favorite things	Talking about favorite things	*What are these / those?*	Things students collect	
Lesson 14 Where is it?	Talking about where things are located	*Where's / Where are . . . ?* *It's not / They're not . . .*	Objects in a bedroom	
Lesson 15 Connections	Reading • Listening Writing			

Unit 4 – Around Town

Lesson	Function	Grammar	Vocabulary	Theme Project
Lesson 16 At the movies	Asking where someone is	*Are you . . . ?*	Places in town	Make a guide of useful places in your town or city for visitors.
Lesson 17 Downtown	Describing where something is	*Is it . . . ?*	More places in town Locations	
Lesson 18 At the mall	Talking about where people are	*Is she / Are they . . . ?*	Places in the mall	
Lesson 19 Any suggestions?	Making suggestions	Suggestions for others Suggestions for you + others	At the beach	
Lesson 20 Connections	Reading • Listening Writing			

Unit 5 – Family and Home

Lesson	Function	Grammar	Vocabulary	Theme Project
Lesson 21 My family	Talking about family members	*have / has*	Numbers 21–100 Family members	Make a group photo album.
Lesson 22 Family reunion	Describing what someone is like	*What's . . . like?*	Appearance and personality traits	
Lesson 23 My new city	Describing new neighborhoods and friends	*We're / They're; Our / Their*	Adjectives to describe places and people	
Lesson 24 At home	Describing a home	*It has . . .*	Areas of a house	
Lesson 25 Connections	Reading · Listening Writing			

Unit 6 – At School

Lesson	Function	Grammar	Vocabulary	Theme Project
Lesson 26 The Media Center	Talking about what is in a room	*There's / There are . . . There's no / There are no . . .*	Things in a media center	Make a poster of a community center.
Lesson 27 Around school	Asking about school facilities	*Is there a / Are there any . . . ?*	School facilities	
Lesson 28 School subjects	Describing a class schedule	*on / at*	School subjects Saying the time	
Lesson 29 Spring Day	Talking about time and when events begin	*What time . . . ?*	Special events	
Lesson 30 Connections	Reading · Listening Writing			

Unit 7 – Around the World

Lesson	Function	Grammar	Vocabulary	Theme Project
Lesson 31 People and countries	Talking about where people are from	*is / isn't; are / aren't in short answers*	Countries	Make an informational guide about people and customs around the world.
Lesson 32 Nationalities	Describing famous people	*isn't / aren't in statements*	Nationalities	
Lesson 33 Holidays	Talking about holidays	*When is . . . ?*	Months of the year Holidays	
Lesson 34 Important days	Describing favorite months	*in / on*	Dates and ordinal numbers	
Lesson 35 Connections	Reading · Listening Writing			

Unit 8 – Teen Time

Lesson	Function	Grammar	Vocabulary	Theme Project
Lesson 36 Favorite places	Talking about favorite places	*What's it like?*	Adjectives to describe places	Make a bookmark of healthy foods and activities.
Lesson 37 Talent show	Describing talents	*can / can't*	Talents	
Lesson 38 School fashion	Talking about school uniforms	*What color is / are . . . ?*	Clothing Colors	
Lesson 39 Teen tastes	Talking about likes and dislikes	*love / like / don't like*	Music Food	
Lesson 40 Connections	Reading · Listening Writing			

Classmates

1. Saying hello

A It is the first day of school at Kent International School. Listen and practice.

Hi. I'm Nicole.

Hi. I'm Jenny.

Hello. I'm Yoshi.

Hi. My name is Paulo.

Hello. My name is Sandra.

Hello. I'm Tyler.

B Play a chain game. Learn your classmates' names.

Sara Hi. My name is Sara.
Robert Hello, Sara. I'm Robert.
    Robert Hi. My name is Robert.
    Victor Hi, Robert. My name is Victor.
      Victor Hi. I'm . . .

2. Language focus

A Jenny and Paulo meet. Listen and practice.

Jenny   Hi. I'm Jenny.
        What's your name?
Paulo   My name is Paulo.
Jenny   Nice to meet you, Paulo.
Paulo   Nice to meet you, too.

> **What's your name?**
>
> **What's your name?**
>   **My name is** Paulo.
> **I'm** Jenny.
>
> *What's = What is*   *I'm = I am*

B Complete the conversations. Listen and check.
   Then practice.

1. **Jenny** What's _your_ (you / your) name?
   Sandra _____ (My / Your) name is Sandra.

2. **Yoshi** Hello. _____ (I'm / You) Yoshi.
   Paulo Nice to meet _____ (you / your), Yoshi.

3. **Nicole** I'm Nicole. _____ (Is / What's) your name?
   Tyler _____ (My / You) name is Tyler.

4. **Sandra** Hi. My _____ (nice / name) is Sandra.
   Yoshi _____ (My / I'm) Yoshi. Nice to meet you.

3. Speaking

Introduce yourself to three classmates.

      You Hello. I'm .... What's your name?
Classmate My name is ....
      You Nice to meet you, ...
Classmate Nice to meet you, too.

2 Hello.

1. Greetings

🔊 Samantha greets people. Listen and practice.

1

Good morning, Samantha.

Sorry I'm late, Mr. White.

2

Good afternoon, Mrs. Morgan.

Hello, Samantha.

3

Good evening, Miss Clark.

Hi, Samantha.

Titles		Single	Married
Females	**Miss**	☑	☐
	Mrs.	☐	☑
	Ms.	☑	☑
Males	**Mr.**	☑	☑

2. Listening

🔊 Which greetings do you hear? Listen and check (✓) two greetings for each conversation.

	Good morning.	Good afternoon.	Good evening.	Hi.	Hello.
Conversation 1	☐	☑	☐	☐	☑
Conversation 2	☐	☐	☐	☐	☐
Conversation 3	☐	☐	☐	☐	☐
Conversation 4	☐	☐	☐	☐	☐

3. Language focus

🔊 **A** Ms. Davis and Sandra greet each other. Listen and practice.

Ms. Davis	Good morning, Sandra. How are you today?
Sandra	Fine, thank you. How about you?
Ms. Davis	Great, thanks. Are you ready for the new school year?
Sandra	Yes, I am.

B Study the language chart.

How are you?		
How are you?		
Great.	**Fine. Good. OK. Not bad.**	**Not too good.**

🔊 **C** Complete the conversations with the words in the boxes. Listen and check. Then practice.

☑ are ☐ Not ☐ too ☐ you

1. **Tyler** Good morning. How ___are___ you?
   Sandra _____ bad, thanks.
   How about _____ ?
   Tyler Not _____ good.

☐ afternoon ☐ Good ☐ How ☐ you

2. **Ms. Davis** Good _____ , Paulo.
   How are you today?
   Paulo OK. _____ about you?
   Ms. Davis _____ , thank _____ .

4. Speaking

Greet three classmates.

Good .... How are you?   .... How about you?

Mini-review

1. Language check

Complete the conversations with the sentences in the box.
Then practice.

> ☐ Hi, Emily. ☐ Nice to meet you, Michael. ☑ What's your name?
> ☐ How are you? ☐ Not bad.

First day of school

Second day of school

Emily Hi. I'm Emily. *What's your name?*

Michael My name is Michael.

Emily _____

_____

Michael _____

Emily Hello, Michael. _____

Michael Good, thanks. How about you?

Emily _____

2. Listening

◁)) **A** What's next? Listen and check (✓) the correct response.

1. ☐ Great, thanks.
   ☑ I'm Joseph.

2. ☐ Thank you.
   ☐ Good morning.

3. ☐ Fine, thanks.
   ☐ My name is Jennifer.

4. ☐ Not too good.
   ☐ Nice to meet you.

5. ☐ Hello, Dan. Sorry I'm late.
   ☐ How about you?

6. ☐ Good evening, Elizabeth.
   ☐ Nice to meet you, too.

◁)) **B** Now listen to the complete conversations. Check your answers.

3. Game Maze Races

A How fast can you connect the words in the maze to make four sentences?

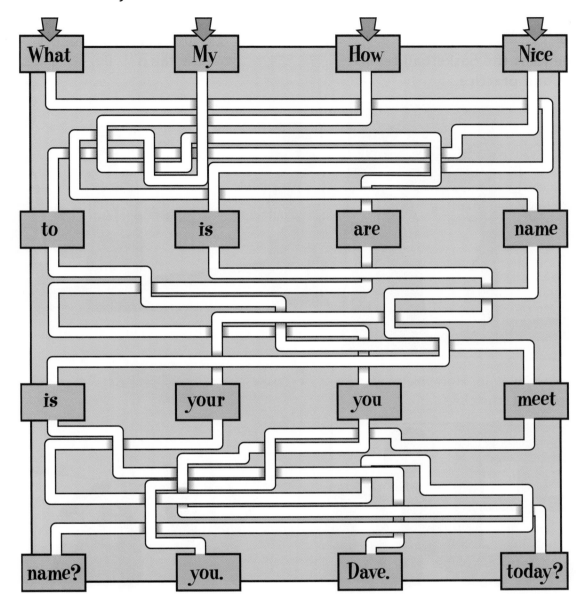

B Complete the conversations with the sentences from part A.

1. **A** _____

   B _____

2. **A** _____

   B Nice to meet you, too.

3. **A** _____

   B Great!

C Now practice with a classmate. Use your own information.

> What is your name?   My name is ....

1. Language focus

🔊 **A** Nicole joins the basketball team. Listen and practice.

> **this is (name)**
> Mr. Diaz, **this is** Nicole Martel.
> Nicole, **this is** Mr. Diaz.

Tyler Mr. Diaz, this is Nicole Martel.

Tyler Hi, Nicole. How are you?
Nicole Good, thanks.

Tyler Nicole, this is Mr. Diaz.
Nicole Hi, Mr. Diaz. Nice to meet you.
Mr. Diaz Nice to meet you, too.

Mr. Diaz OK. Are you ready? Let's go!

B Introduce two classmates to each other.

You ...., this is ....
........, this is ....
Classmate 1 Hi, ...
Classmate 2 Hi, ... Nice to meet you.

C Complete the conversations with the words in the box.
Which conversation is an introduction? Circle it.

☐ are   ☐ Good   ☐ Hello   ☑ is   ☐ you

1. **Mr. Diaz** Hi, Jenny.
   Jenny Hi, Mr. Diaz. This ___*is*___ Paulo Santos.
   Paulo Nice to meet _____ , Mr. Diaz.

2. **Tyler** _____ , Sandra.
   Sandra Hi, Tyler. How _____ you?
   Tyler _____ , thanks.

2. Listening

Are these conversations introductions?
Listen and check (✓) Yes or No.

	Yes	No		Yes	No
Conversation 1	☑	☐	Conversation 4	☐	☐
Conversation 2	☐	☐	Conversation 5	☐	☐
Conversation 3	☐	☐			

3. Saying good-bye

A Listen and practice.

B Play a chain game. Say good-bye to your classmates.

Ken Good-bye, Elena.
Elena See you later, Ken.

  Elena Bye, Mina.
  Mina Bye-bye, Elena.

    Mina See you tomorrow, . . .

Lesson 4 Names

1. Vocabulary

◁)) **A** Listen to these common American names. Then practice.

Girls' names		Boys' names	
Amanda	Jessica	Andrew	Joseph
Ashley	Katherine	Christopher	Joshua
Elizabeth	Megan	Daniel	Matthew
Emily	Samantha	David	Michael
Jennifer	Sarah	Jacob	Nicholas

◁)) **B** Listen to the alphabet. Then practice.

A B C D E F G H I J K L M N O P Q R S T U V W X Y Z

a b c d e f g h i j k l m n o p q r s t u v w x y z

◁)) **C** How do these students spell their names?
Listen and write the names. Then practice.

Ashley   _____   _____   _____   _____

2. Pronunciation Syllables

◁)) **A** Study the pronunciation chart. Then listen and practice.

1 syllable	2 syllables	3 syllables
Dan	Ash ley	Chris to pher

◁)) **B** Listen to these names. How many syllables do they have?

1. Emily _3_   2. Joe ___   3. Jacob ___   4. Katherine ___   5. David ___

3. Language focus

◁ **A** Adriana gets a library card.
   Listen and practice.

Mr. Moore What's your name?
Adriana Adriana Moraes.
Mr. Moore Is that A-D-R-I-A-N-A?
Adriana Yes, that's right.
Mr. Moore And how do you spell
   your last name?
Adriana M-O-R-A-E-S.
Mr. Moore OK. Here's your card.
Adriana Thank you.

Names	
First names	**Last names**
Yoshi	Sato
Jenny	Wilson
Tyler	Foster
How do you spell your last name?	
M-O-R-A-E-S.	

Kent International School

Adriana Moraes

4   020   11209   00012

LIBRARY CARD
for books, CDs, and videos

B Complete the conversation with
   your own information. Then practice.

A What's your name?

B _____

A How do you spell your last name?

B _____

4. Speaking

Play a chain game. Learn to spell your classmates' names.

Robert How do you spell your first name, Ken?
Ken K-E-N.

→ **Ken** How do you spell your last name, Sara?
Sara R-I-V-E-R-A.

→ **Sara** How do you spell your first name, . . . ?

Connections

1. Reading

International E-Mail Club Guestbook

Are nicknames common in your country? Do you have a nickname?

Amanda	Francisco	Su Wei
Hi. My name is Amanda. My nickname is Mandy. This is my dog, Polo. His nickname is Po.	Good morning. I'm Francisco. My nickname is Chico. I'm great today! How are you?	Hello. My name is Su Wei. My nickname is Wei Wei. My last name is Chan. Nice to meet you!

A Read about the e-mail club members.

B Read about the club members again. Write the nicknames for these names.

Name	Nickname		Name	Nickname
1. Amanda	_____		3. Francisco	_____
2. Polo	_____		4. Su Wei	_____

C Write the nicknames for these names. Use the names next to the chart.

Name	Nickname		Name	Nickname
1. Christopher	*Chris*		6. Megan	_____
2. Jennifer	_____		7. Joseph	_____
3. Michael	_____		8. Elizabeth	_____
4. Katherine	_____		9. Andrew	_____
5. Nicholas	_____		10. Jessica	_____

- ☐ Andy
- ☐ Jess
- ☐ Mike
- ☐ Kate
- ☐ Meg
- ☐ Liz
- ☑ Chris
- ☐ Jenny
- ☐ Joe
- ☐ Nick

2. Listening

🔊 It is the first day of computer class. Listen to the conversations, and complete the information.

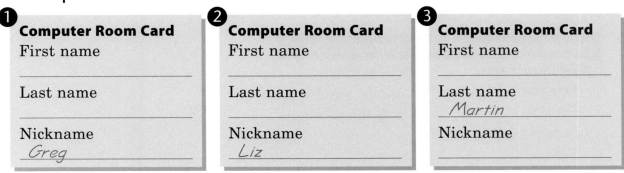

① Computer Room Card

First name
_____

Last name
_____

Nickname
Greg

② Computer Room Card

First name
_____

Last name
_____

Nickname
Liz

③ Computer Room Card

First name
_____

Last name
Martin

Nickname
_____

3. Writing

A Jenny joins an international e-mail club.
Read her application and her message.

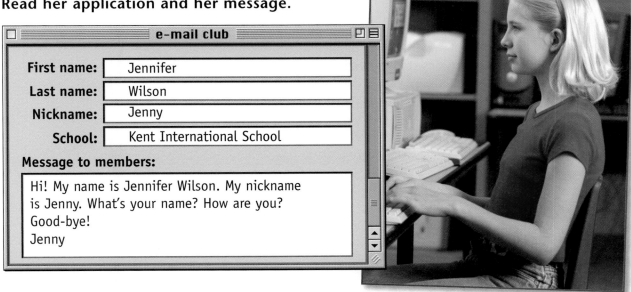

e-mail club

First name: Jennifer

Last name: Wilson

Nickname: Jenny

School: Kent International School

Message to members:

Hi! My name is Jennifer Wilson. My nickname
is Jenny. What's your name? How are you?
Good-bye!
Jenny

B Complete your own application. Then write a message.
Use ideas from the box or your own ideas.

e-mail club

First name: _____

Last name: _____

Nickname: _____

School: _____

Message to members:

_____

How are you?
Hi.
What's your name?
Good morning.
What's your nickname?
Hello.
Good-bye.

Language chart review

Personal information	Introductions
What's your name? **My name is** Emily. **I'm** Emily. **How do you spell** your name? E-M-I-L-Y. **How are you** today? **Great!** **Fine**, thank you. **Not too good.**	Hi. **I'm** Emily. Andrew, **this is** Meg. Meg, **this is** Andrew.
What's = What is *I'm = I am*	

A Complete the conversations with the sentences in the box.

☑ Hello, Mr. McDonald. How are you? ☐ Nice to meet you, too.
☐ Monica, this is Steven. ☐ Not bad, thank you.

1. **A** *Hello, Mr. McDonald. How are you?*

   B Good, thanks. How about you, Caroline?

   A _____

2. **A** _____

   B Hi, Steven. Nice to meet you.

   C _____

B Match the conversations from part A to the pictures.
Write the numbers.

C Meet Sara and Sarah. Complete the conversations.

1 Hello. *What's* your name?

INTERNATIONAL CLUB

My name _____ Sara Smith.

Hi. _____ Sarah, too.

2 How do you spell _____ name?

S-A-R-A-H. _____ about you?

S-A-R-A.

3 Hi, Sarah. _____ are you today?

Great, thanks. Mr. Lopes, _____ is my new friend, Sara.

4 Hi, Sara. _____ to meet you.

Nice to meet _____, too, Mr. Lopes.

D Circle the word in each box that is different. Then complete the message with the colored letter from that word.

(Hello.)	Good morning.	Not bad.	David
Good night.	Good-bye.	Great.	Jacob
Bye.	Good afternoon.	Thank you.	Megan
Good-bye.	Good evening.	Fine.	Nicholas

S e e   y   u   l   t   r !

Teachers and friends

1. Vocabulary

A Listen to Tyler talk about his photo album. Number the pictures.
Then listen again and practice.

This is my *best friend*, Paulo.

This is my
classmate, Jenny.

This is my *math*
teacher, Mr. Stern.

This is my *science*
teacher, Ms. Davis.

1

This is my *basketball*
coach, Mr. Diaz.

This is my *computer partner*, Sandra.

B Write about three people at your school.

<u>Ms. Davis is my science teacher.</u>

2. _____

1. _____

3. _____

2. Language focus

🔊 **A** Tyler and his dad look at photos.
Listen and practice.

Tyler Look, Dad, this is my new
basketball coach.
Mr. Foster What's his name?
Tyler His name is Mr. Diaz.
Mr. Foster Who's this?
Tyler This is my computer partner.
Her name is Sandra.
Mr. Foster And who's this?
Tyler Dad! This is Paulo – my best friend.

his / her
What's **his** name?
His name is Mr. Diaz.
What's **her** name?
Her name is Sandra.

Who's this?
Who's this?
This is my computer partner.
My computer partner.
Who's = Who is

🔊 **B** Complete the conversations. Listen and check. Then practice.

1. **Mr. Foster** ___Who's___ (Who's / What's) this?
   Tyler My math teacher.
   Mr. Foster What's _____ (his / her) name?
   Tyler _____ (His / Her) name is Mr. Stern.

2. **Tyler** This is my classmate.
   Mr. Foster _____ (What's / Who's) her name?
   Tyler _____ (His / Her) name is Jenny.

3. **Mr. Foster** And _____ (who's / what's) this?
   Tyler My science teacher. _____ (His / Her) name is Ms. Davis.

3. Pronunciation Contractions with question words ····•

🔊 **A** Listen. Notice the contractions *Who's* and *What's*. Then listen again
and practice.

Who's this?	What's her name?	What's his name?

B Now practice the conversations in 2B.

Favorite stars

1. Vocabulary

🔊 **Look at the photos in Sandra's scrapbook. Label the pictures with the words in the box. Then listen and practice.**

☐ actor ☑ model ☐ soccer player ☐ TV star
☐ cartoon character ☐ singer ☐ tennis player

1 Gisele Bündchen
model

2 Anna Kournikova

3 Spider-Man

4 Ronaldo

5 Alicia Keys

6 Brad Pitt

7 Carson Daly

2. Language focus

He's/She's...

He's my favorite soccer player.
She's my favorite model.

He's = He is   *She's = She is*

A Nicole and Sandra talk about their favorite stars. Listen and practice.

Nicole Who's this?
Sandra Gisele Bündchen. She's my favorite model.
Nicole And who's this?
Sandra Ronaldo. He's my favorite soccer player.
Nicole So, who's your favorite actor?
Sandra Brad Pitt. He's right here.
Nicole Oh, I'm a Brad Pitt fan, too. I think he's cute.

B Write about these stars from Sandra's scrapbook. Then listen and check.

1. (Gisele Bündchen) *This is Gisele Bündchen. She's a model.*

2. (Spider-Man) _____

3. (Anna Kournikova) _____

4. (Carson Daly) _____

5. (Ronaldo) _____

3. Listening

Listen to students talk about their favorite stars. Check (✓) the correct stars.

1. ☑ actor   2. ☐ model   3. ☐ soccer player   4. ☐ cartoon character
   ☐ TV star   ☐ singer   ☐ tennis player   ☐ TV star

4. Speaking

Complete the chart with your favorite stars.
Then ask two classmates about their favorite stars.

	You	Classmate 1	Classmate 2
Actor	_____	_____	_____
Singer	_____	_____	_____
Cartoon character	_____	_____	_____

Who's your favorite .... ?   My favorite .... is ....

Mini-review

1. Language check

A Meg introduces Pat to Jacob. Complete the conversation. Then practice.

Meg Hi, Jacob. How ___are___ (is / are) you?
Jacob Great, thanks.
Meg Jacob, _____ (this / she) is Pat.
_____ (He's / She's) my science partner.
Jacob Nice to meet _____ (you / she), Pat.
Pat Nice to meet you, too. _____ (What's / Who's) your science partner, Jacob?
Jacob Rebecca.
Pat _____ (What's / Who's) her last name?
Jacob Johnson.
Pat Really? She's _____ (my / your) best friend!

B Complete the sentences with *He's*, *She's*, *His*, or *Her*.

Pat   Meg   Jacob

This is Nick. ___He's___ my computer partner. _____ favorite class is math.

This is Lauren. _____ my best friend. _____ favorite singer is Madonna.

Mr. Benson is my favorite teacher. _____ great. _____ first name is Charlie.

2. Game Word Search

A Can you find these people in the puzzle? Circle the words.
Look in these directions (→ ↓ ↘).

- ☐ actor
- ☑ best friend
- ☐ classmate
- ☐ coach
- ☐ math teacher
- ☐ model
- ☐ singer
- ☐ soccer player

q	s	a	k	y	b	j	g	b	m	u	o
p	b	u	v	i	e	s	t	q	r	p	n
c	s	m	b	z	s	x	i	w	i	m	s
l	o	k	o	u	t	l	c	n	l	o	m
a	n	a	t	k	f	h	w	v	g	d	n
s	o	c	c	e	r	p	l	a	y	e	r
s	d	u	z	h	i	a	i	t	d	l	r
m	a	t	h	t	e	a	c	h	e	r	s
a	t	e	q	i	n	k	t	t	f	e	d
t	c	a	v	p	d	x	i	h	o	r	q
e	i	s	j	k	i	v	e	t	s	r	r

B Now label the pictures.

1. _best friend_
2. _____
3. _____
4. _____
5. _____
6. _____
7. _____
8. _____

8 Birthday party

1. Numbers 0–20

🔊 **A** Listen to the numbers. Then practice.

0 zero (oh)
1 one
2 two
3 three
4 four
5 five
6 six
7 seven
8 eight
9 nine
10 ten
11 eleven
12 twelve
13 thirteen
14 fourteen
15 fifteen
16 sixteen
17 seventeen
18 eighteen
19 nineteen
20 twenty

🔊 **B** Look at the picture. Listen and write the ages.

1. Lisa and Steve are ___twelve___ .
2. Beth is _____ .
3. Ashley is _____ .
4. Matt is _____ .
5. Jessica is _____ .

2. Language focus

◁)) **A** Lisa is at Steve's birthday party.
Listen and practice.

How old ...?	
How old are you?	**How old is she?**
I'm twelve.	**She's** three.

He's not / She's not	
He's not thirteen. He's twelve.	
She's not four. She's only three.	

Lisa   Happy birthday, Steve!
How old are you? Thirteen?

Steve   No, I'm twelve.

Lisa   I'm twelve, too. Your little
sister, Ashley, is so cute.
How old is she? Four?

Steve   No, she's not four. She's only three.

◁)) **B** Look at 1B on page 22. Answer the questions. Then listen and check.

1. How old is Steve? Thirteen? _No, he's not thirteen. He's twelve._

2. How old is Jessica? Twelve? _____

3. How old is Lisa? Eleven? _____

4. How old is Ashley? Six? _____

5. How old is Matt? Ten? _____

6. How old is Beth? Eighteen? _____

3. Listening

A How old are the other people at the party?
Write your guesses in the chart.

	Chris	Anna	Andy	Joshua
Your guess	eleven			
Correct age				

◁)) **B** Compare answers. Then listen and write the correct ages in the chart.

> How old is Chris? I think he's eleven.

> I think he's thirteen.

4. Speaking

Play a chain game. Learn the ages of your classmates.

Mina   How old are you, Robert?

Robert   I'm thirteen.

      → Robert   How old are you, Sara?

Sara   I'm twelve.

      → Sara   How old are you, ...?

Favorite People   23

Lesson 9 E-pals

1. Vocabulary

🔊 **A** Jenny and Paulo look at students and their e-pals.
Where are they from? Listen and complete the sentences.
Then listen again and practice.

1. Paulo is from ___*Brazil*___ .   His e-pal is from ___*Peru*___ .

2. Jenny is from _____ .   Her e-pal is from _____ .

3. Nicole is from _____ .   Her e-pal is from _____ .

4. Tyler is from _____ .   His e-pal is from _____ .

5. Sandra is from _____ .   Her e-pal is from _____ .

6. Yoshi is from _____ .   His e-pal is from _____ .

B Now draw lines to match the students with their e-pals.

Students

Canada

United States

Sandra, Mexico
(age 12)

Mexico

Venezuela

Colombia

Paulo, Brazil
(age 12)

Peru

Brazil

E-pals

Mike, Canada
(age 12)

Miguel, Colombia
(age 12)

2. Speaking

Talk about the people on the map.

        You Mike is from Canada.
Classmate 1 How old is he?
Classmate 2 He's twelve.

3. Language focus

A Paulo and Jenny talk about e-pals.
Listen and practice.

Paulo Hi, Jenny. Who's that?
Jenny That's Mike. He's my e-pal. He's twelve.
Paulo Where's he from?
Jenny He's from Canada.
Paulo You're from Canada, too, right?
Jenny Canada? I'm not from Canada.
Paulo Really? Where are you from?
Jenny I'm from the U.S.
Paulo Oh, right. Sorry.

Where . . . from?
Where are you from?   **I'm from** the U.S.
Where's he from?   **He's from** Canada.
Where's = Where is
You're / I'm not
You're from Canada, right?   **I'm not** from Canada.   I'm from the U.S.
You're = You are
the U.S. = the United States

Jenny, **the U.S.**
(age 13)

Portugal

Tyler, **the U.S.**
(age 12)   Japan

Nicole, **Canada**
(age 12)

Yoshi, **Japan**
(age 12)

María, **Peru**
(age 13)

Emma, **Australia**
(age 13)

Australia

Claudio, **Venezuela**
(age 14)

Lina, **Portugal**
(age 13)

B Complete the conversation. Listen and check. Then practice.

Paulo Here's a photo of my e-pal, María.
Jenny She's cute! _____ she from?
Paulo _____ from Peru.
Jenny Peru? You're from Peru, too, right?
Paulo Jenny, I'm _____ from Peru. I'm from Brazil.
Jenny I'm just kidding! I know that.

Connections

1. Reading

Do you have friends in other countries? Where are they from?

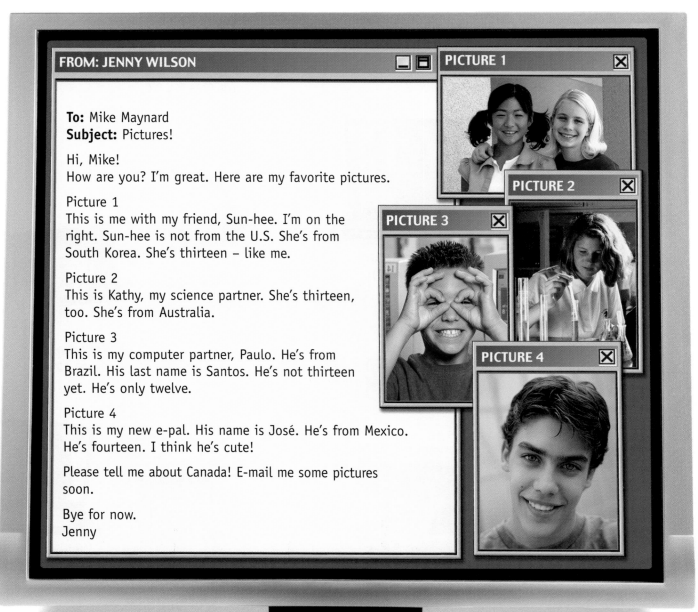

FROM: JENNY WILSON

To: Mike Maynard
Subject: Pictures!

Hi, Mike!
How are you? I'm great. Here are my favorite pictures.

Picture 1
This is me with my friend, Sun-hee. I'm on the right. Sun-hee is not from the U.S. She's from South Korea. She's thirteen – like me.

Picture 2
This is Kathy, my science partner. She's thirteen, too. She's from Australia.

Picture 3
This is my computer partner, Paulo. He's from Brazil. His last name is Santos. He's not thirteen yet. He's only twelve.

Picture 4
This is my new e-pal. His name is José. He's from Mexico. He's fourteen. I think he's cute!

Please tell me about Canada! E-mail me some pictures soon.

Bye for now.
Jenny

PICTURE 1

PICTURE 2

PICTURE 3

PICTURE 4

A Read Jenny's message to her e-pal, Mike.

B Complete the chart about the people in Jenny's e-mail.

	Name	Country	Age
Her friend	*Sun-hee*	*South Korea*	*thirteen*
Her science partner			
Her computer partner			
Her new e-pal			

2. Listening

🔊 Now listen to Mike's message to Jenny. Who are these people?
Check (✓) the correct words.

Mr. Smith
☐ soccer coach
☐ tennis coach

Krissy
☐ computer partner
☐ science partner

Tony Edison
☐ favorite actor
☐ favorite TV star

Angela Vargas
☐ favorite singer
☐ favorite model

3. Writing

A Read José's first message to Jenny.

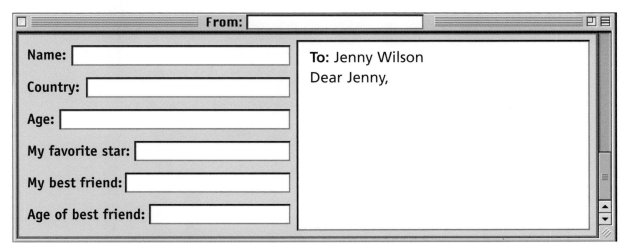

```
═══════════════ From: José Rivera ═══════════════
To: Jenny Wilson
Dear Jenny,
My name is José Rivera. My nickname is Pepe. I'm fourteen years old. I'm from
Mexico City, Mexico. My favorite actor is Salma Hayek. She's from Mexico, too.
She's great. My best friend is Peter Rodriguez. He's thirteen.
Who's your favorite star? Who's your best friend?
Please write soon.
Pepe
```

B Complete the information about yourself. Then write a message to Jenny.

From: _____

Name: _____

Country: _____

Age: _____

My favorite star: _____

My best friend: _____

Age of best friend: _____

To: Jenny Wilson

Dear Jenny,

Lessons 6-10 Review

Language chart review

The verb *be*			
Wh- questions	**Statements**	**I'm / He's / She's . . .**	**My / His / Her . . .**

How old are you?	**I'm** 16.
	    I'm not 18.
	 You're 15.
	    You're not 14.
		I'm a singer.
		 He's a model.
		 She's a teacher.
			My name is Carla.
			 His name is Steven.
			 Her name is Ms. Kelly.

Where's he from?	**He's** from Brazil. **He's not** from Peru.	*He's = He is* *She's = She is*	
Where's she from?	**She's** from Canada. **She's not** from France.		
Who's this?	**This is** my best friend.		
Where's = Where is *Who's = Who is*	*You're = You are*		

A Complete the sentences in the comic book with *I'm*, *he's*, *she's*,
my, *his*, or *her*.

B Complete the questions with *Who, What, Where,* or *How.*
Then match each question to the correct answer.

1. _How_ old is Katrina? _f_
2. _____ is she from? ____
3. _____ is her best friend? ____
4. _____ old is Mira? ____
5. _____ is Kegar from? ____
6. _____ is the name of his school? ____

a. She's from Earth.
b. Mira.
c. He's from Andor.
d. She's fourteen.
e. The Andor School for Space Travel.
f. She's thirteen.

C Read about these comic book characters. Then write about them.

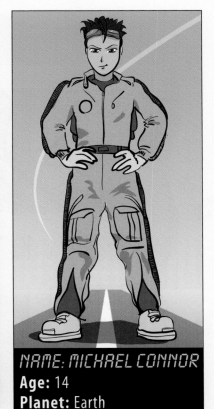

NAME: MAGNUM TOR
Age: 15
Planet: Andor

NAME: DANU ZENOD
Age: 17
Planet: Nexus

NAME: MICHAEL CONNOR
Age: 14
Planet: Earth

1. _His name is Magnum._

   He's _____ .

   He's _____ .

2. _____

   _____

   _____

3. _____

   _____

   _____

D Look again at part C. Correct these sentences.

1. Magnum is sixteen.   _Magnum is not sixteen. He's fifteen._
2. You're from Nexus.   _____
3. Danu is fifteen.   _____
4. Danu is from Andor.   _____
5. Michael is from Nexus. _____
6. You're twenty.   _____

What a mess!

1. Vocabulary

🔊 **A** Lucy and Mark are home from school. Label their things with the words in the box. Then listen and practice.

- ☐ address book
- ☐ bag
- ☐ brush
- ☐ eraser
- ☐ notebook
- ☐ pencil case
- ☑ backpack
- ☐ book
- ☐ camera
- ☐ hat
- ☐ pen
- ☐ umbrella

1. *backpack*
2.
3.
4.
5.
6.
7.
8.
9.
10.
11.
12.

🔊 **B** Look at part A. Listen to Lucy and Mark. Are their statements true or false? Write *T* (true) or *F* (false).

1. Lucy _T_   2. Mark ____   3. Lucy ____   4. Mark ____   5. Lucy ____

Unit 3 Everyday Things

2. Language focus

This is / That's + possessive

This is Lucy's pen.

That's Mark's hat.

That's = That is

🔊 **A** The living room is a mess.
Listen and practice.

Mrs. West	Mark!
Mark	Yes, Mom?
Mrs. West	Look at your things! What a mess!
Mark	My things? This is Lucy's pen, and that's her book.
Lucy	Yes, but that's Mark's hat, and . . .

🔊 **B** Complete Mark's and Lucy's sentences with *This is* or *That's*.
Then listen and check.

This is Mark's camera.
That's Mark's pencil case.
_____ Mark's notebook.
_____ Mark's bag.
_____ Mark's brush.

_____ Lucy's eraser.
_____ Lucy's umbrella.
_____ Lucy's backpack.
_____ Lucy's address book.

3. Speaking

Talk about your classmates' things.

This is Roberto's pencil case.   That's Anna's . . .

Lesson 12 Cool things

1. Vocabulary

A Complete the sentences with the words in the box.
Then listen and practice.

☐ an alarm clock	☐ a cell phone	☐ an electronic organizer	☑ a TV (television)
☐ a calculator	☐ a computer	☐ a radio	☐ a video game

1

This is __a TV__ . That's _____ .

2

This is _____ . That's _____ .

3

This is _____ . That's _____ .

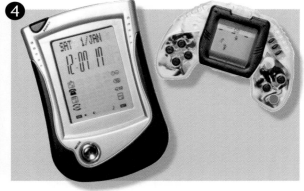

4

This is _____ . That's _____ .

B Write *a* or *an* before each word.

1. _an_ address book
2. ____ basketball
3. ____ camera
4. ____ pencil case
5. ____ eraser
6. ____ hat
7. ____ umbrella
8. ____ video game

a / an
a + consonant
a TV
a radio
an + vowel sound
an alarm clock
an electronic organizer

C Listen to the sounds. What do you hear?
Who can answer first?

> That's an alarm clock.

2. Language focus

◁》 A Sandra and Jenny look at interesting things. Listen and practice.

What's this / that?	
What's this?	**What's that?**
It's a cell phone.	**It's** a video game.
It's = It is	

Sandra Hey, Jenny. What's this?
A cell phone?

Jenny No, it's a calculator.

Sandra Hmm. It's weird.
And what's that?

Jenny It's a video game.

Sandra Wow! It's really cool.

◁》 B Complete the conversations with the words in the box.
Listen and check. Then practice.

☐ a	☐ camera	☐ It's	☐ this	☑ What's
☐ an	☐ cool	☐ that	☐ weird	

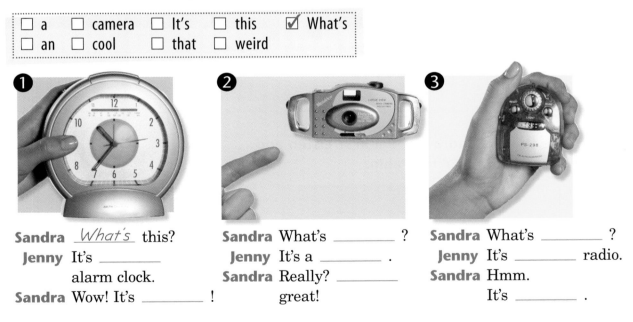

❶

Sandra _What's_ this?

Jenny It's _____
alarm clock.

Sandra Wow! It's _____ !

❷

Sandra What's _____ ?

Jenny It's a _____ .

Sandra Really? _____
great!

❸

Sandra What's _____ ?

Jenny It's _____ radio.

Sandra Hmm.
It's _____ .

3. Listening

◁》 What things do Tyler and Yoshi talk about? Listen and circle
the correct things.

1. TV / computer
2. calculator / electronic organizer
3. cell phone / video game
4. alarm clock / radio

Mini-review

1. Language check

These classmates are at the Museum of Technology. What do they say?
Write sentences with *This is* or *That's*.

1. **Terry:** *That's a phone.*

2. **Melissa:** _____

3. **Suzanne:** _____

4. **Joe:** _____

2. Listening

Are these things Sandra's or Paulo's? Listen and
write *S* for Sandra or *P* for Paulo.

1. _____P_____

2. _____

3. _____

4. _____

5. _____

6. _____

3. Game What's This?

A What are these objects? Guess. Label each photo.

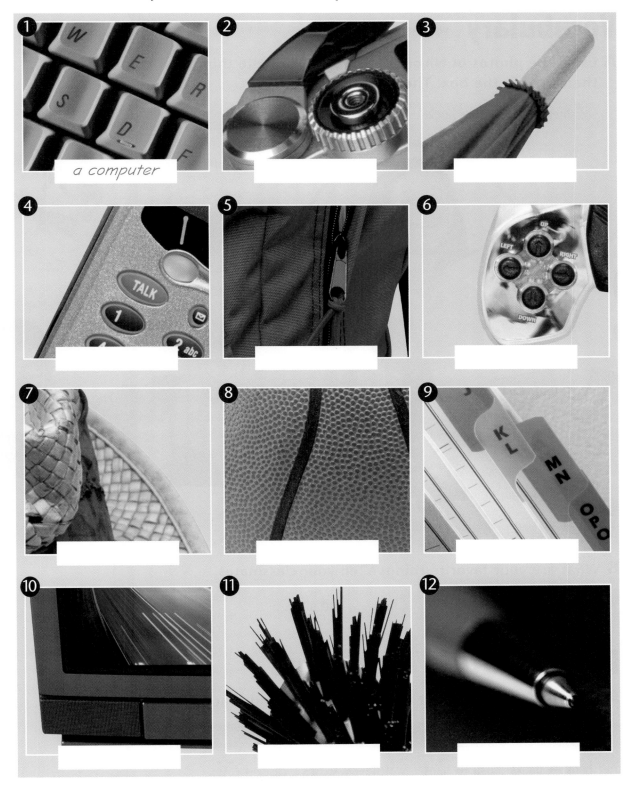

1 _a computer_

2

3

4

5

6

7

8

9

10

11

12

B How many of your answers are correct? Compare with a classmate.

> **You** What's this?
> **Classmate** I think it's a computer.
> **You** I think it's a television.

Favorite things

1. Vocabulary

A Label the photos of Nicole's and Yoshi's favorite things with the words in the box. Then listen and practice.

☑ bicycle ☐ comic books ☐ posters ☐ trading cards ☐ T-shirts ☐ watch

① bicycle

②

③

④

⑤

⑥

B What are your favorite things? Tell your classmates.

My favorite things are my . . . , my . . . , and my . . .

2. Pronunciation Plural nouns

A Study the pronunciation chart. Then listen and practice.

No extra syllables		Extra syllable	
book → books	bag → bags	watch → watches	case → cases

B Listen. Which plural nouns have extra syllables? Circle them.

1. hats
2. games
3. (coaches)
4. friends
5. brushes
6. boxes

3. Language focus

A It's Collectors' Day at school. Listen and practice. Then study the language chart.

Mr. Park Hi, Alexis. Tell me about your collections. What are these?

Alexis They're my favorite T-shirts.

Mr. Park Oh, they're interesting. And what are those?

Alexis Those are posters of my favorite singers.

Mr. Park Singers? Hmm. They're, uh . . . nice. Thank you, Alexis.

What are these / those?	
What are these?	**What are those?**
These are T-shirts.	**Those are** posters.
They're T-shirts.	**They're** posters.
They're = They are	

B Look at the picture. Complete the conversation with *these*, *those*, or *they're*. Listen and check. Then practice.

Ms. Rios So, what are ___those___ , Simon?

Simon They're my favorite comic books.

Ms. Rios Hmm. _____ very interesting.

Simon _____ are my trading cards.

Ms. Rios Oh, _____ nice. What's in this box?

Simon Look inside. _____ are my favorite friends.

Ms. Rios Simon, _____ snakes!

Simon Yeah. They're great pets.

4. Speaking

Look at the things in the pictures on pages 36 and 37. Ask and answer questions.

What are these?	They're T-shirts.	What's this?	It's a / an . . .

Everyday Things 37

Lesson 14 — Where is it?

1. Vocabulary

A David is late for school. Where are his things?
Match the two parts of each sentence. Then listen
and practice.

1. David's books are __c__
2. His basketball is ____
3. His brush is ____
4. His watch is ____
5. His bag is ____

a. under the bed.
b. in the wastebasket.
c. on the desk.
d. on the dresser.
e. next to the chair.

in

under

next to

on

dresser
bed
chair
desk
wastebasket

B Look at David's room. Complete the sentences with
in, *under*, *next to*, or *on*.

1. David's alarm clock is __on__ the dresser.
2. His hat is _____ the bed.
3. His wastebasket is _____ the desk.
4. His computer is _____ the desk.
5. His books are _____ the camera.
6. His pencils are _____ the bag.

the

the desk
the books

38   Unit 3

2. Language focus

🔊 **Complete the conversation. Listen and check. Then practice.**

David Dad! I'm late. Where are my pencils? They're not in my pencil case.

Mr. Evans They're in your bag.

David OK, but where's my bag? It's not on the desk.

Mr. Evans It's under the bed.

David Oh, right. Thanks. Oh! *Where are* my books? _____ in my bag.

Mr. Evans _____ next to your computer.

David And _____ my watch? _____ on the dresser.

Mr. Evans _____ in the wastebasket, David!

Where's / Where are . . . ?
Where's my bag?
It's under the bed.
Where are my pencils?
They're in your bag.

It's not / They're not . . .
It's not on the desk.
They're not in my pencil case.

3. Listening

🔊 **Where's the backpack? Listen and number the pictures.**

 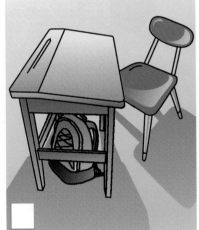

4. Speaking

Look at the picture on page 38. Write one true statement and one false statement. Read your statements. Your classmates say *Yes* or *No*.

1. The bag is under the bed.

2. The books are next to the desk.

You The bag is under the bed.
Classmate 1 Yes.
You The books are next to the desk.
Classmate 2 No. They're not next to the desk. They're on the desk.

1. Reading

What are your favorite things? Do you have any collections?

Collection Club News

I'm Kate Burns. I'm 12 years old. I'm from Australia. I collect clocks. I have more than 35 clocks. They're not expensive, and they're really cool. This is my favorite clock – it's a cat!

I'm Elena Lucas. I'm from Mexico. I'm 12 years old. My favorite things are my lunch boxes. I have a big lunch-box collection. Some are really old, and some are new. I think they're great.

I'm John Black from the U.S. I'm 13, and I'm a trading-card collector. These are my trading cards from Japan, Brazil, and Australia. International trading cards are fun!

A Read the articles in the Collection Club News.

B Are these sentences true or false? Check (✓) T (true) or F (false).

	T	F
1. The trading-card collector is from the U.S.	✓	
2. Elena and John are the same age.		
3. Clocks are expensive in Australia.		
4. The lunch-box collector is 12 years old.		
5. Kate has a favorite clock.		

2. Listening

◁》 **A** Listen to an interview with another collector, Marco.
Check (✓) the correct words.

Country	**Age**	**Collection**
☐ Brazil	☐ twelve	☐ comic book collection
☐ Peru	☐ thirteen	☐ movie collection

B Now complete the interview with the
questions in the box.

┌───┐
│ ☐ What are these?   ☐ Where's she from? │
│ ☐ What's this?   ☐ Who's this?   │
└───┘

Interviewer So, tell me about your collection.

_____

Marco It's my favorite movie, *Star Wars*.

Interviewer _____

Marco They're my favorite movie posters.

Interviewer _____

Marco She's my favorite actor.
Her name is Salma Hayek.

Interviewer _____

Marco She's from Mexico.

3. Writing

Write an article about your favorite things. Use 1A to help you.

Name: _____

Age: _____

Country: _____

Favorite things: _____

My name is . . .

Review

Language chart review

this / that / these / those questions and statements *a / an*	
This is a camera.	**These are** pens.
What's this? **It's a** camera.	**What are these?** **They're** pens.
That's an address book.	**Those are** comic books.
What's that? **It's an** address book.	**What are those?** **They're** comic books.
That's = That is *It's = It is*	*They're = They are*
Possessive 's	
This is Paul**'s** backpack. These are Eva**'s** pencils.	

A Ben and Lee are at camp. Look at the picture. Then complete the conversation.

Lee Hey, Ben. What are _____*those*_____ (these / those) ?

Ben _____ (It's / They're) my favorite comic books.

Lee Who's _____ (that / those) ?

Ben _____ (It's / They're) the Joker.

He's _____ (a / an) *Batman* character.

Lee Oh, right. He's not _____ (Batman / Batman's) friend.

And _____ (what's / who's) that?

Ben It's _____ (a / an) electronic organizer.

Lee Wow! It's really small. And what's _____ (this / that)

in your backpack?

Ben _____ (It's / They're) my new camera.

B The names of seven more things are in the pencil. Circle them.
Then write them in the chart. Use *a* or *an* for the singular words.

watch umbrellacomicbookscamerascellphonebicycleaddressbooksposters

Singular	Plural
a watch	

Language chart review

Where's / Where are . . . ?		Prepositions
Where's my cell phone?	**It's not** in my bag.	**in**
	It's on the desk.	**on**
Where are my books?	**They're not** next to my computer.	**next to**
	They're under the table.	**under**

C Look at the picture. Then correct the sentences.

1. The books are on the desk. *They're not on the desk. They're on the bed.*

2. The pencils are next to the backpack. _____

3. The umbrella is next to the dresser. _____

4. The hat is on the bed. _____

D Look again at the picture in part C. Write questions and answers
about the other things.

1. **Q:** *Where's the basketball?*   **A:** *It's next to the dresser.*

2. **Q:** _____   **A:** _____

3. **Q:** _____   **A:** _____

4. **Q:** _____   **A:** _____

At the movies

1. Vocabulary

◁)) Where are Jenny and her friends? Match the two parts of
each sentence. Then listen and practice.

1. Jenny is ___c___   a. at the newsstand.
2. Tyler is _____   b. at the restaurant.
3. Sandra is _____   c. at the movie theater.
4. Nicole is _____   d. at the Internet café.
5. Yoshi is _____   e. at the bus stop.
6. Paulo is _____   f. at the shoe store.

at
at the newsstand

Jenny

Tyler

Sandra

Nicole

Yoshi

Paulo

2. Listening

◁)) Look at the photos in 1. Where are the people?
Listen and number the places.

☐ Internet café   ☐ newsstand   1 restaurant   ☐ movie theater   ☐ shoe store   ☐ bus stop

3. Language focus

Are you ...?

Are you still at home?
Are you near the movie theater?
Yes, I am.
No, I'm not.

A Jenny is at the movie theater. All of her friends are late! Listen and practice.

Tyler Hello?
Jenny Tyler, this is Jenny. It's really late. Are you still at home?
Tyler No, I'm not.
Jenny Oh. Are you near the movie theater?
Tyler Yes, I am. I'm at the bus stop.
Jenny Well, please hurry. You're late!
Tyler OK. I'm sorry.

B Complete the conversations. Listen and check. Then practice.

1. **Sandra** Hello?
   Jenny Hi, Sandra. Where are you? Are ___you___ near the movie theater?
   Sandra Yes, I _____ . I'm at the shoe store.
   Jenny _____ you with Paulo?
   Sandra No, I'm _____ .
   Jenny OK. Hurry. It's late!

2. **Paulo** Hello?
   Jenny Hi, Paulo. You're late! _____ _____ near the movie theater?
   Paulo No, _____ _____ . I'm still at home.
   Jenny Oh, no, Paulo! Hurry!
   Paulo I'm kidding. I'm at the newsstand.

4. Speaking

Complete these questions. Then interview a classmate.

Are you ...?	Yes	No
Are you _____ years old? (*age*)	☐	☐
Are you a _____ player? (*sport*)	☐	☐
Are you a _____ fan? (*favorite star*)	☐	☐
Are you from _____ ? (*city* or *town*)	☐	☐

Are you 12 years old?

Yes, I am.

Lesson 17 Downtown

1. Vocabulary

A Look at the map. Complete the sentences. Then listen and practice.

1. The drugstore is _____*on*_____ Jefferson Street.
2. The department store is _____ the movie theater.
3. The parking lot is _____ the movie theater.
4. The bank is _____ the restaurant and the shoe store.
5. The subway station is _____ the shoe store.
6. The park is _____ the school.

on

in front of

behind

across from

between

B Look at the places on the map. Make true and false statements. A classmate answers *True* or *False*.

The parking lot is behind the movie theater.   True.

2. Language focus

🔊 **A** Liz and Rosa are downtown.
Listen and practice.

Liz I'm hungry! Let's go
to Tom's Restaurant.
Rosa OK. Where is it?
Liz I think it's on Park Avenue.
Rosa Oh. Is it across from
the Internet café?
Liz No, it's not. It's next to the bank.
Rosa But the bank is
on Jefferson Street.
Liz Uh-oh. I'm lost!
Let's look at the map!

> **Is it . . . ?**
>
> **Is it** across from the Internet café?
> **Yes, it is.**
> **No, it's not.**

B Write four questions about the map on page 46.
Then practice with a classmate.

1. *Is the parking lot behind the shoe store?*
2. _____
3. _____
4. _____
5. _____

> Is the parking lot behind the shoe store?

> No, it's not. It's behind the movie theater.

3. Pronunciation *Yes / No* questions

🔊 Listen. Notice the intonation in the questions.
Then listen again and practice.

A Is the school on Park Avenue?
B Yes, it is.

A Is the restaurant in front of the drugstore?
B No, it's not.

4. Speaking

Think of a place in your town or city. Your classmates guess the place.

Classmate 1 Is it near the school?
You Yes, it is.
Classmate 2 Is it on Miller Avenue?
You No, it's not.

Classmate 3 Is it across from the school?
You Yes, it is.
Classmate 4 Is it the park?
You Yes, it is.

1. Language check

A Carlos and Anna are at a soccer game. Complete the conversations with *I am, I'm not, it is,* or *it's not.* Then practice.

Carlos Hi. Are you Anna Jones?
Anna Yes, __/__ __am__ .
Carlos I'm in your science class.
Anna Oh, right. . . . GO, TIGERS, GO!
Carlos Are you from Canada, Anna?
Anna Uh, no, _____ _____ .
I'm from the U.S.
Carlos Are you on a soccer team?
Anna No, _____ _____ . I'm just
a fan. GO! GO!
(Ring! Ring!)
Carlos Anna, is that your cell phone?
Anna Oh! Yes, _____ _____ . Thanks.

Anna Hello?
Mrs. Jones Anna, are you still at school?
Anna Uh, no, _____ _____ .
A GOAL! YAY, TIGERS!
Mrs. Jones Anna, are you at the
soccer field?
Anna Well, yes, _____ _____ .
Is that OK?
Mrs. Jones No, _____ _____ !
It's very late.
Anna But, Mom, . . .

B Complete these questions. Then practice with a classmate.

1. __Are__ you a soccer fan?
2. _____ you 12 years old?
3. _____ your English class interesting?
4. _____ you a good student?
5. _____ your school nice?
6. _____ your home near the school?

Are you a soccer fan?   No, I'm not.

2. Game Find the Differences

How is Picture 2 different from Picture 1? Complete the chart.

Picture 1

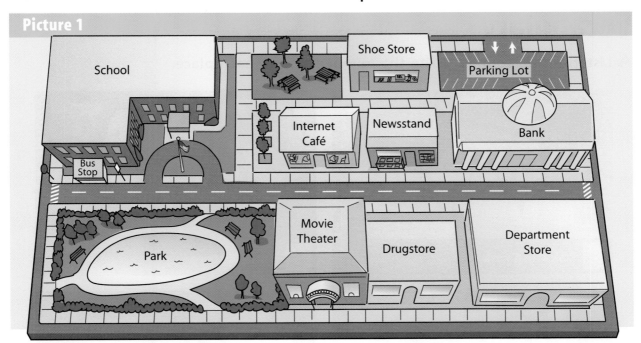

Picture 2

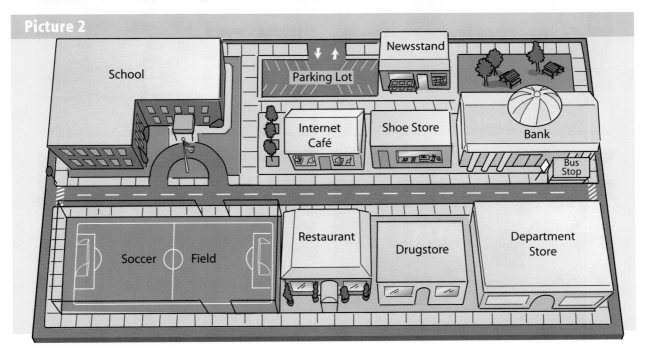

Picture 1	Picture 2
The bus stop is in front of the school.	*The bus stop is in front of the bank.*
The school is across from the park.	
The parking lot is behind the bank.	
The newsstand is in front of the shoe store.	
The drugstore is between the movie theater and the department store.	

18 At the mall

1. Vocabulary

A Listen to the sounds. Write the number next to each place.

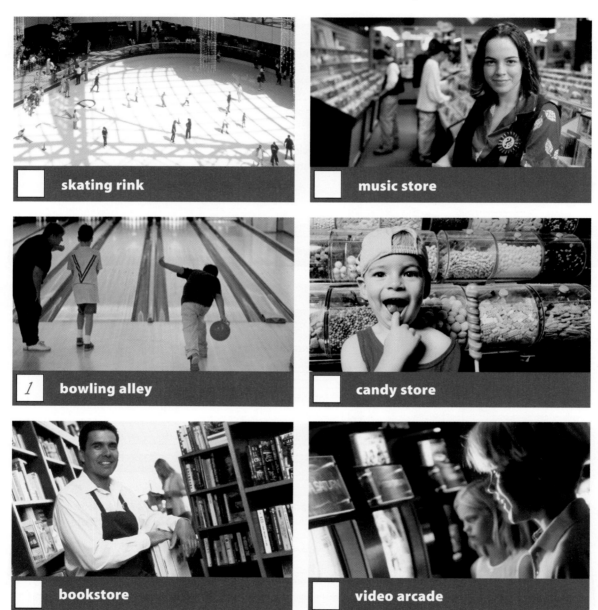

	skating rink		music store
1	bowling alley		candy store
	bookstore		video arcade

B Listen and check. Then practice.

C Write about three of your favorite places.

My favorite music store is Virgo Beat Music.

1. _____

2. _____

3. _____

2. Language focus

Is she / Are they . . . ?

Is she at the video arcade?
  Yes, she is.
  No, she's not.
Are they at the skating rink?
  Yes, they are.
  No, they're not.

A Yoshi and Paulo are at the mall
   with their friends. Listen and practice.

Yoshi Where is everybody?
Paulo Well, Tyler and Jenny are
       at the video arcade.
Yoshi What about Nicole?
       Is she there, too?
Paulo No, she's not. She's with Sandra.
Yoshi Oh. Are they at the skating rink?
Paulo No, they're not. . . . They're at the
       movie theater.
Yoshi Oh, no! Let's hurry!

B Read the conversation again. Complete
   the questions and then answer them.
   Then listen and check.

1. (Yoshi) _____ *Is he* _____ with Nicole?
   _____ *No, he's not.* _____
2. (Jenny) _____ at the video
   arcade? _____
3. (Yoshi and Paulo) _____ at
   the mall? _____
4. (Tyler) _____ with Yoshi?
   _____
5. (Nicole) _____ with Tyler
   and Jenny? _____
6. (Nicole and Sandra) _____
   at the skating rink? _____

3. Listening

A It's two hours later. Where are Paulo and his friends now?
   Listen and check (✓) the correct places.

	Candy store	Music store	Bookstore	Video arcade
Paulo	☐	☐	☐	☐
Jenny	☐	☐	☐	☐
Tyler	☐	☐	☐	☐
Nicole	☐	☐	☐	☐

B Compare answers with a classmate.

Is Paulo at the music store?   No, he's not. He's at the ･･･････ .

Lesson 19 Any suggestions?

1. Vocabulary

🔊 **A** Look at the people at the beach. Listen to the suggestions and practice.

Go swimming.

Go to a café.

Play volleyball.

FOOD SHACK

Have a sandwich.

Sit down.

Have a soda.

BEACH

B Now write a suggestion for each person below. Use part A to help you.

I'm tired.	**I'm thirsty.**	**I'm hungry.**	**I'm hot.**	**I'm bored.**
Sit down.				

2. Listening

🔊 What's the problem with these people? Listen and check (✓) the correct problem.

1. ☐ She's hot.
   ☐ She's tired.

2. ☐ He's bored.
   ☐ He's hungry.

3. ☐ They're thirsty.
   ☐ They're hungry.

4. ☐ She's tired.
   ☐ She's bored.

3. Language focus

◁)) A Matt and Chris are at the beach.
Listen and practice.

Suggestions for others
Have a soda.
Suggestions for you + others
Let's go together.

Matt I'm thirsty.
Chris So go to a café, and
have a soda.
Matt Good idea, but, um . . .
Chris What's wrong?
Matt Well, my money is at home.
Chris That's OK. I have money for
two sodas. Let's go together.
Matt Great! Thanks, Chris!

◁)) B Complete the conversations with *go, have, sit,* or *play.*
Listen and check. Then practice.

1. **A** Let's __*play*__ basketball.
   B But it's really hot.
   A Yeah – you're right.
   Let's _____ to the beach.
   B Good idea. Let's _____
   swimming.

2. **A** I'm tired.
   B So _____ down.
   A OK. But I'm thirsty, too.
   B Then _____ to a café,
   and _____ a soda.

3. **A** Let's _____ a sandwich.
   I'm hungry.
   B Well, I'm not really hungry,
   but I am thirsty!
   A Oh. So _____ a soda.
   B OK. Let's _____ to a café.

4. **A** I'm really bored.
   B Me, too. Let's _____
   to a video arcade.
   A But my money is at home.
   B Then let's _____ tennis
   in the park.
   A OK.

4. Speaking

Make suggestions. Use your own information or ideas.

I'm ·······.   So ·······.   I'm ·······.   Me, too. Let's ·······.

Connections

1. Reading

What's your favorite Saturday activity? Where do you go?

Saturday Suggestions

Carlos – Rio de Janeiro, Brazil

Go to Ipanema Beach. Play volleyball or go swimming in the Atlantic Ocean. Look at the people. Everybody is happy. It's my favorite place.

Michiko – Tokyo, Japan

Go to a department store in Shibuya. Shibuya is a great shopping area in Tokyo. Sometimes it's very crowded, but that's OK – I love shopping!

Lise – Paris, France

Go to the Eiffel Tower. It's really tall. Look at the river and the beautiful buildings. The view of Paris is great.

Jason – New York City, USA

Go to the skating rink in Central Park. Look at the ice-skaters. They're good! Or, go skating yourself. It's really fun!

🔊 **A** Read the article. Which is your favorite suggestion? Tell your classmates.

B Read the article again. Then answer the questions.

1. Is Shibuya in Paris? _No, it isn't._
2. Are the ice-skaters in Central Park good? _____
3. What is the name of Carlos's favorite place? _____
4. Is Michiko a shopping fan? _____
5. Where is Carlos from? _____
6. Is the Eiffel Tower in France? _____
7. Is Central Park in Tokyo? _____

2. Listening

 Are these suggestions for others or the speaker and others?
Listen and check (✓) the correct information.

	1	2	3	4	5	6
Others	☐	☐	☐	☐	☐	☐
Speaker and others	☑	☐	☐	☐	☐	☐

3. Writing

An e-pal plans to visit your town or city. Where should she go?
Look at the example. Then complete the chart, and write a message.

Place	park
Location	First Street
Activity	swim in the pool
Why	It's fun.

Place	
Location	
Activity	
Why	

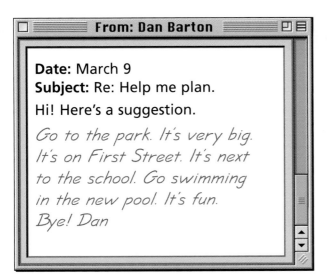

From: Dan Barton

Date: March 9
Subject: Re: Help me plan.

Hi! Here's a suggestion.

_Go to the park. It's very big.
It's on First Street. It's next
to the school. Go swimming
in the new pool. It's fun.
Bye! Dan_

From:

Date: March 9
Subject: Re: Help me plan.

Hi! Here's a suggestion.

Review

Language chart review

Yes / No questions and short answers with *be*			Prepositions
Are you near the restaurant?	Yes, **I am.**	No, **I'm not.**	**on**
Is Yoshi at the video arcade?	Yes, **he is.**	No, **he's not.**	**in front of**
Is Sandra with Tyler?	Yes, **she is.**	No, **she's not.**	**across from**
Is the café near the movie theater?	Yes, **it is.**	No, **it's not.**	**behind**
Are Jenny and Paulo at the café?	Yes, **they are.**	No, **they're not.**	**between**

A Write questions with the correct forms of *be*. Then look at the picture, and answer the questions.

1. the school / behind the park

   Q: *Is the school behind the park?*   **A:** *No, it's not.*

2. the bicycles / behind the school

   Q: _____   **A:** _____

3. the soccer field / across from the park

   Q: _____   **A:** _____

4. the parking lot / in front of the school

   Q: _____   **A:** _____

5. the school / between the tennis courts and the soccer field

   Q: _____   **A:** _____

6. the school / on International Street

   Q: _____   **A:** _____

B Look at the pictures. Complete the questions and answers.

1.  **Q:** _Are they_ at the restaurant?

   A: _Yes, they are._

2.  **Q:** _____ at the movie theater?

   A: _____

3.  **Q:** _____ at the newsstand?

   A: _____

4.  **Q:** _____ at the café?

   A: _____

5.  **Q:** _____ at the bus stop?

   A: _____

Language chart review

Suggestions for others	Suggestions for you + others
Play volleyball.	**Let's go** swimming.
Sit down.	**Let's sit** on the sofa.
Have a soda.	**Let's watch** a movie.

C Write a suggestion for each situation. Use the expressions in the box or your own ideas.

☐ go   ☐ go swimming   ☑ have a soda   ☐ sit and watch TV   ☐ sit down

1. You and your friends are thirsty. _Let's have a soda._

2. Your brother is tired. _____

3. You and your sister are late for a movie. _____

4. Your friend is hot. _____

5. You and your friends are tired. _____

My family

1. Numbers 21–100

🔊 **Listen to the numbers. Then practice.**

21 twenty-one	**22** twenty-two	**23** twenty-three
24 twenty-four	**25** twenty-five	**26** twenty-six
27 twenty-seven	**28** twenty-eight	**29** twenty-nine

30	**40**	**50**	**60**	**70**	**80**	**90**	**100**
thirty	forty	fifty	sixty	seventy	eighty	ninety	one hundred

2. Vocabulary

🔊 **A** Meet Emily's family. Listen and practice.

My name is Emily. I'm 13.

These are my grandparents. My grandfather is 74. My grandmother is 67.

These are my parents. My father is 50. His name is Joe. My mother is 46. Her name is Barbara.

This is my aunt, Susan, and my uncle, Bill. She's 38 and he's 39.

This is my brother, David. He's 15. This is my sister, Sarah. She's 21.

This is my cousin, Michael. He's 13, like me.

B Complete these sentences about Emily's family.

1. Emily's ___mother___ is 46.
2. Her father is _____ .
3. Her _____ is 13.
4. Her aunt is _____ .
5. Her _____ is 15.
6. Her sister is _____ .
7. Her _____ are 67 and 74.
8. Her _____ is 39.

3. Language focus

🔊 **A** Meet Emily's cousin. Listen and practice.

I'm Michael. I'm Emily's cousin. Emily has a brother and a sister, so I have three cousins. But I have no brothers or sisters – I'm an only child.

have / has
I **have** three cousins. I **have** no brothers or sisters. She **has** a brother and a sister. He **has** no brothers.
cousin → cousins   child → children

🔊 **B** Complete the sentences with *have* or *has*. Then listen and check.

My name is Bill. I'm Emily's uncle. I *have* one sister. Her name is Barbara. She's Emily's mother. She _____ three children – Sarah, David, and Emily. I _____ one child, Michael.

I'm Emily's grandmother. I _____ two children – Barbara and Bill. Barbara _____ three children. Bill _____ one child.

4. Speaking

A Complete the information for yourself. Then complete the information about a classmate.

Relative	You
brother(s)	_____
sister(s)	_____
cousin(s)	_____
aunt(s)	_____
uncle(s)	_____

I have two brothers.

I have no brothers.

Relative	Classmate
brother(s)	_____
sister(s)	_____
cousin(s)	_____
aunt(s)	_____
uncle(s)	_____

B Tell the class one thing about you and your classmate.

I have two brothers. Maria has no brothers.

Lesson 22 Family reunion

1. Vocabulary

A Read about Sally's family. Then listen and practice.

B Read about Sally's family again. What words describe the people? Write the words in the correct columns.

Appearance	Personality
handsome	friendly

2. Language focus

What's . . . like?
What's Pam like?
She's shy.

A Sally and Dan talk about her family. Complete the conversation. Listen and check. Then practice.

Sally That's Pam. She's my cousin.
Dan What's she like?
Sally She's shy and . . .
Dan She's very pretty.
Sally Yes, I know, Dan.
Dan What's your brother _____ ?
Sally Tom? Oh, _____ smart.
Dan And your Aunt Edna? _____ she _____ ?
Sally Well, _____ really funny and a little _____, too!

B Complete the chart about two members of your family. Then answer a classmate's questions about those family members.

Family member	Appearance	Personality
sister	tall	shy

Sister.   What's your sister like?   She's tall and shy.

3. Pronunciation Final *y*

Listen to the pronunciation of final *y* in two-syllable words. Then listen again and practice.

cra**zy**   fun**ny**   pret**ty**   friend**ly**   real**ly**

4. Listening

A What else is true about Sally's family? Listen and match the two parts of each sentence.

1. Sally's mother is tall and ____   a. funny.
2. Sally's cousin, Henry, is handsome and ____   b. a little crazy.
3. Sally's grandfather is friendly and ____   c. thin.
4. Sally's father is short and really ____   d. smart.

B Now ask and answer questions about Sally's family.

What's Sally's mother like?   She's tall and . . .

Mini-review

1. Language check

A Nicole talks to Yoshi about her family. Complete the sentences with *have* or *has*.

I _have_ a very big family. I _____ four sisters and three brothers. My mother _____ three brothers, too. My father _____ no brothers, but he _____ five sisters. I _____ 18 cousins. It's great!

B Compare your family to Nicole's family. Tell your classmates.

> Nicole has four sisters. I have no sisters.

2. Listening

A Now listen to Nicole describe three members of her family. Label the photos.

☐ Robert ☐ Andrew ☐ John

_____   _____   _____

B Complete the chart with information about three members of your family. Then tell your classmates.

Name	Family member	Age	Description
Peter	cousin	16	tall, thin, very smart

> My cousin's name is Peter. He's 16. He's . . .

3. Game Who's This?

A Look at Ralph's family tree. Who are the people in his family?

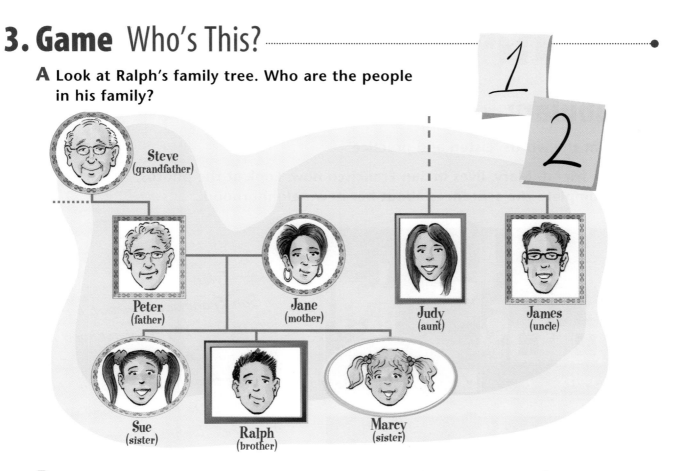

B Play the game with a classmate. Use things in your bag as game markers.

- Close your eyes and touch one of the numbers. Move your game marker that number of spaces.
- **Classmate 1:** Ask "Who's this?" and point to the name in the box.
  Classmate 2: Answer "He's / She's Ralph's . . ."

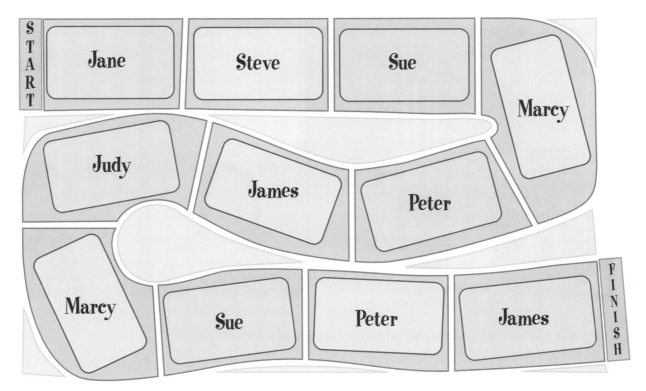

23 My new city

1. Vocabulary

🔊 **A** Look at the words. Listen and practice.

B Tyler's friend, Mary, lives in San Francisco now. Look at the photos, and complete the sentences about her new neighborhood.

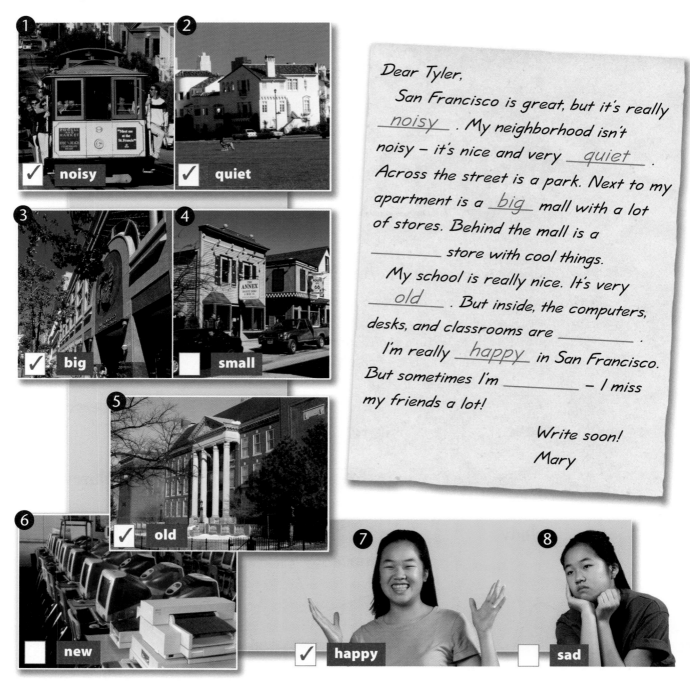

1. ✓ noisy
2. ✓ quiet
3. ✓ big
4. ☐ small
5. ✓ old
6. ☐ new
7. ✓ happy
8. ☐ sad

Dear Tyler,

San Francisco is great, but it's really _noisy_ . My neighborhood isn't noisy – it's nice and very _quiet_ . Across the street is a park. Next to my apartment is a _big_ mall with a lot of stores. Behind the mall is a _____ store with cool things.

My school is really nice. It's very _old_ . But inside, the computers, desks, and classrooms are _____ .

I'm really _happy_ in San Francisco. But sometimes I'm _____ – I miss my friends a lot!

Write soon!

Mary

C Tell your classmates about your neighborhood.

> My neighborhood is quiet.

2. Language focus

Tyler sends a postcard to Mary. Complete Tyler's postcard with *we're, they're, our,* or *their.* Listen and check. Then practice.

We're / They're; Our / Their
We're happy for you.
They're from Canada.
Our neighbors are very nice.
Their last name is Martel.
We're = We are They're = They are

Dear Mary,

Thanks for the letter. We miss you, too. But *we're* happy for you. San Francisco is a great city.

The Martels live in your house now. ________ from Canada. ________ family is big. ________ all very nice. Nicole Martel and I are in the same English class. *Our* English teacher is her father, Mr. Martel!

Nicole is also on my basketball team. ________ team is really great this year. ________ number one! Two players are from Brazil. ________ names are Carlos and Sergio. ________ really good.

Write soon. I miss you a lot!

Tyler

Mary Clark
123 Park Lane
San Francisco, CA
94109

3. Listening

A The Martels talk about where they live. Listen and check (✓) the correct words.

1. the city	☐ nice	☑ big	☑ noisy
2. the neighborhood	☐ pretty	☐ quiet	☐ small
3. the neighbors	☐ happy	☐ quiet	☐ friendly
4. the house	☐ small	☐ nice	☐ new
5. the school	☐ big	☐ small	☐ noisy

B Now compare where you live to where the Martels live. Write three sentences.

Their city is big. Our city is small.

1. ______________________________

2. ______________________________

3. ______________________________

1. Vocabulary

A Which room is Brandon in? Listen and write the numbers.

B Listen and check. Then practice.

C Where are these things? Answer the questions.

1. Where is Brandon's poster collection? *It's in the bedroom.*

2. Where is his bicycle? _____

3. Where are his comic books? _____

4. Where is his backpack? _____

5. Where is his hat? _____

6. Where are his shoes? _____

2. Language focus

It has...

It has a small yard.
It has three bedrooms.

◁)) **A** Match the homes to the correct texts.
Listen and check. Then practice.

☐ This is my grandparents' house. It's in the country. It has three bedrooms. It has a small yard.

☐ Our apartment is small, but it's very nice. It has two bedrooms and one bathroom. It has a big kitchen and a nice living room.

☐ My friend has a very big house. It has five bedrooms and three bathrooms! It also has a big garage.

B What's your home like? Write sentences with *It's* and *It has*.

_____

_____

_____

_____

3. Speaking

A What's your dream home like? Check (✓) your ideas.

My dream home is . . .
☐ a house
☐ an apartment

It's . . .
☐ in the city
☐ in the country

It's . . .
☐ big
☐ small

It has . . .
☐ a living room
☐ a dining room
__ bathroom(s)
__ bedroom(s)

It has . . . , too.
☐ a yard
☐ a garage
☐ a kitchen
☐ a/an _____

The neighborhood is . . .
☐ noisy
☐ quiet
☐ nice

B Now tell your classmates.

My dream home is a house. It's in the country. It's . . .

Lesson 25 Connections

1. Reading

What's unusual about these houses? What other kinds of houses do you know?

Unusual Houses

A house? A boat? A houseboat!

Pete and Karen Clay are from Kentucky. They have an unusual home. It's a houseboat named Fargo. Their houseboat has a living room, a dining room, a kitchen, a bathroom, and three bedrooms. The Clays' children, Andy and Kris, love it. "It's a cool house and a fun boat," says Kris.

Up in a tree!

Grant Stone is 12, and his sister, Jenna, is 8. They're only kids, but they have a house. It's a tree house! It's in the country. It's at their grandparents' house in Kansas. Their tree house has one room. It's a living room with a table and a few chairs. It's small, but Grant and Jenna think it's great. Grant says, "It's my favorite place! That's the name – My Place."

🔊 **A** Read the article about the houses.

B Read the article again. Then complete the chart.

Name	Kind of home	Name of home	Location	Number of rooms
The Clays	_____	_____	_____	_____
The Stones	_____	_____	_____	*1*

C Are these sentences true or false? Check (✓) T (true) or F (false).

	T	F
1. The Clays' houseboat has two bedrooms.	☐	☑
2. The Clays' houseboat is small.	☐	☐
3. Grant is 12 years old.	☐	☐
4. Grant has two sisters.	☐	☐
5. The tree house is big.	☐	☐

2. Listening

🔊 Now listen to Grant describe another home.
Check (✓) what he says.

Kind of home	Location	Size	Number of rooms	His bedroom
☑ apartment	☐ in the country	☐ big	☐ six	☐ nice
☐ house	☐ in the city	☐ small	☐ seven	☐ noisy

3. Writing

Write an article about your home.
Use the questions to help you.

What kind of home is it? (an apartment / a house)
Where is it? (in the country / in the city)
What's it like? (big / small / new / old)
How many bedrooms?
How many bathrooms?
What is your bedroom like? (nice / small)

My home is . . .

_____

_____

_____

Language chart review

has / have statements	We're / They're; Our / Their	What's . . . like?
I **have** two sisters. I **have** no brothers. He **has** a big family. She **has** an apartment. It **has** one bedroom.	**We're** from New York. **Our** last name is Diaz. **They're** from Chicago. **Their** last name is Carlton.	**What's** she **like?** She's **nice.**
	We're = We are They're = They are	

A Complete the conversation.

Nina   This is a picture of ___our___ (we / our)
family.

Rick   You and Peter _____ (have / has)
a big family.

Nina   Yeah. We _____ (have / has)
a lot of brothers and sisters.

Rick   Who's this?

Peter   This is _____ (we / our)
brother, Will.

Rick   What's he like?

Peter   _____ (He's / His) smart and
a little shy.

Nina   This is _____ (we / our) aunt,
Ginny, and uncle, Bob.

Peter   _____ (They're / Their) last
name is Richards.

Nina   _____ (They're / Their) really
friendly and nice.

Peter   _____ (They're / Their) from Ohio.

Rick   I'm from New York.

Nina   _____ (We're / Our) from
New York, too!

B Read the conversation again. Answer these questions.

1. What's their brother like? _____

2. What are their aunt and uncle like? _____

3. Where is their uncle from? _____

4. Where are Nina and Peter from? _____

C Complete the sentences with the words in the box.

☐ Her ☐ His ☑ my ☐ My ☐ Our ☐ Their ☐ your

I'm Bobby Parker. This is __my__ father. _____ name is Tom. _____ mother's name is Beverly. I have one sister. _____ name is Jane. I have two brothers, too. _____ names are Mike and Joe. _____ family is pretty big. What's _____ family like?

D Write about your family. Use some of the words from part C.

I'm . . . _____

_____

_____

E What's the difference? Compare Amy's house and Ben's house. Write sentences with *has* and *has no*.

Amy's house

Kitchen
Living room
Bedroom
Dining room
Bedroom
Bathroom
Bedroom
Bathroom

Ben's house

Garage
Kitchen
Living room
Bedroom
Bathroom
Bedroom

1. (bedroom) _Amy's house has three bedrooms._
   Ben's house has two bedrooms.

2. (living room) _____

_____

3. (bathroom) _____

_____

4. (dining room) _____

_____

5. (kitchen) _____

_____

6. (garage) _____

_____

Lesson 26 The Media Center

1. Vocabulary

A Label the things in the new media center with the words in the box. Then listen and practice.

☑ board	☐ cabinet	☐ CD player	☐ screen
☐ bookcase	☐ cassette player	☐ printer	☐ VCR (video cassette recorder)

1. *board*

Welcome to the Media Center!

2.
3.
4.
5.
6.
7.
8.

Unit 6 At School

B Ask and answer questions about things in your classroom.

What's that?   It's a board.   What are those?   They're computers.

72

2. Language focus

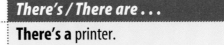

There's / There are . . .

There's a printer.
There are six computers.

There's no / There are no . . .

There's no wastebasket.
There are no chairs.

There's = There is

🔊 **A** There is a problem in the media center.
Listen and practice.

Mr. Smith So, here's the new media center.
Ms. Lane Wow! It's great.
Mr. Smith Wait a minute. . . .
There's a problem.
Ms. Lane What's wrong?
Mr. Smith Well, there are only six computers.
Ms. Lane Oh, dear. Well, there's a printer.
Is that right?
Mr. Smith Yes, that's OK. But there's no wastebasket,
and there are no chairs. Oh, no!

> **Mr. Smith**
> **Hampton Middle School**
>
> ☐ 2 boards   ☐ 1 CD player   ☑ 1 printer
> ☐ 2 bookcases   ☐ 8 chairs   ☐ 1 screen
> ☐ 2 cabinets   ☑ 8 computers   ☐ 1 VCR
> ☐ 1 cassette player ☐ 8 desks   ☐ 1 wastebasket

🔊 **B** Read Mr. Smith's order form. Look at the picture on page 72. What's right?
What's wrong? Write sentences in the correct columns. Then listen and check.

What's right?	What's wrong?
There's a printer.	*There are six computers.*

3. Speaking

Write true or false statements about your classroom.
Read the sentences. Your classmates say *Yes* or *No*.

There's a board. (True)
There are 12 chairs. (False)
There's a wastebasket. (True)

You There's a board.
Classmate 1 Yes.
You There are 12 chairs.
Classmate 2 No. There are 20 chairs.

Around school

1. Vocabulary

🔊 **A** Label the photos of Jenny's school. Then listen and practice.

Kent International School

has a lot!

1. gym
2.
3.

Media Center
- computer lab
  with 50 computers
- language lab

Sports Facilities
- 2 tennis courts
- 4 athletic fields
  * 1 football field
  * 1 baseball field
  * 2 soccer fields
- gym
- swimming pool

Other Facilities
- auditorium
- library
- cafeteria

B Write about the facilities at your school. Use *There is / There are*.

There is . . .

2. Language focus

🔊 **A** Jenny's cousin, Jill, asks about Kent International School. Listen and practice.

Is there a / Are there any . . . ?
Is there a soccer team?
Yes, **there is.**
No, **there isn't.**
Are there any tennis courts?
Yes, **there are.**
No, **there aren't.**
isn't = is not   aren't = are not

Jill Jenny, your school is really great. Are there any tennis courts?
Jenny Yes, there are. There's a tennis team, too.
Jill So, are there any cute players?
Jenny No, there aren't.
Jill Hmm. Is there a soccer team?
Jenny Yes, there is.
Jill Is there a game today?
Jenny No, there isn't. Sorry.

🔊 **B** Complete the rest of the conversation. Listen and check. Then practice.

Jill _Are_ there any other interesting things at your school?
Jenny Yes, there _____ . There are some new classrooms and a new media center.
Jill Oh, that's cool. _____ there an Internet café there?
Jenny No, there _____ .
Jill Hey, I'm hungry. Are there _____ cafés near here?
Jenny No, there _____ . But there's a cafeteria.
Jill Are _____ any cute boys there?
Jenny Yes, there _____ . Let's go!

3. Pronunciation *th*

🔊 **A** Listen to the two pronunciations of *th*. Then listen again and practice.

Voiced			Unvoiced		
there	**th**at	fa**th**er	**th**ree	**th**ink	ba**th**room

🔊 **B** Write these words in the correct columns: *birthday, brother, mother, thanks, the, they, thing, thirty*. Listen and check. Then practice.

Voiced	Unvoiced
_____	_____
_____	_____
_____	_____
_____	_____

At School 75

1. Language check

A Read about the neighborhood around Kent International School.
Then answer the questions.

▶ Enjoy your free time after school!

Bob's Burgers
Hamburgers, sandwiches, and more!
325 Main Street
555-0982

Central Park
56th–60th Streets
Swimming pool
Soccer and baseball fields

City Video Arcade
Your place for after-school fun!
18 South Avenue
555-8722

Kent Shopping Mall
48 stores,
5 movie theaters
25 Park Avenue
555-1618

Lee's Restaurant
Great food from China!
16 West Avenue
555-6723

Maple Bookstore and Internet Café
New and used books
Kent Shopping Mall
555-8655

1. Are there any stores near the school? *Yes, there are.*

2. Are there any athletic fields in the neighborhood? _____

3. Is there a basketball court in the park? _____

4. Is there a bookstore at the mall? _____

5. Are there any restaurants on South Avenue? _____

6. Is there a video arcade in the neighborhood? _____

B Write three sentences about your neighborhood. Then tell your classmates.

There's a park. _____

1. _____

2. _____

3. _____

There's a park. There . . .

2. Game What Do You Remember?

**Look at the picture for one minute. Close your book.
Your teacher asks questions. What do you remember?**

Teacher Are there any tables?
Team A Yes, there are.

Teacher Is there a tennis court?
Team B No, there isn't.

School subjects

1. Vocabulary

🔊 **A** These are some of the classes at Kent International School. Label the books with the words in the box. Then listen and practice.

☐ art   ☐ geography   ☐ history   ☐ music   ☐ science
☑ English   ☐ health   ☐ math   ☐ physical education (P.E.)   ☐ Spanish

① English
hello

②

③

⑦

④

⑤

⑥

⑧

⑨

⑩

B Make a list of your school subjects. Are they easy or difficult for you? Check (✓) Easy or Difficult. Then tell your classmates.

My school subjects	Easy	Difficult
_____	☐	☐
_____	☐	☐
_____	☐	☐
_____	☐	☐
_____	☐	☐

My school subjects	Easy	Difficult
_____	☐	☐
_____	☐	☐
_____	☐	☐
_____	☐	☐
_____	☐	☐

I think geography is easy.

I think math is difficult.

2. Saying the time

🔊 Look at the days and times in Nicole's class schedule.
Listen and practice.

Saying the time
8:30 = eight-thirty
1:05 = one-oh-five
2:00 = two *or* two o'clock

Class Schedule for *Nicole Martel*

	Monday	Tuesday	Wednesday	Thursday	Friday
8:30	English	English	English	English	English
9:25	math	math	math	computer lab	math
10:20	P.E.	health	P.E.	art	P.E.
11:15	lunch	lunch	lunch	lunch	lunch
12:10	history	geography	history	geography	history
1:05	science	science	science lab	science	science
2:00	Spanish	language lab	Spanish	music	Spanish

3. Language focus

on / at
I have computer lab **on** Thursday.
My computer lab is **at** 9:25.

🔊 **A** Nicole talks about her class schedule.
Listen and practice.

This is my school schedule. I have English class every day at 8:30. I think English is easy.

I have history class at 12:10 on Monday, Wednesday, and Friday. History is difficult.

My favorite day is Thursday. I have computer lab at 9:25. It's great!

🔊 **B** Look at Nicole's class schedule in 2 above. Complete the sentences with the day and time. Then listen and check.

1. Nicole's health class is *on Tuesday at 10:20* .

2. Nicole has science lab _____ .

3. Her geography class is _____ .

4. She has Spanish class _____ .

5. Her language lab is _____ .

4. Speaking

What are your three favorite classes at school? When are they?
Tell your classmates.

I think math is great. I have math class on Tuesday at 3:00. I think . . .

Lesson 29 Spring Day

1. Vocabulary

◁)) **A** Look at the Spring Day poster. Listen and practice.

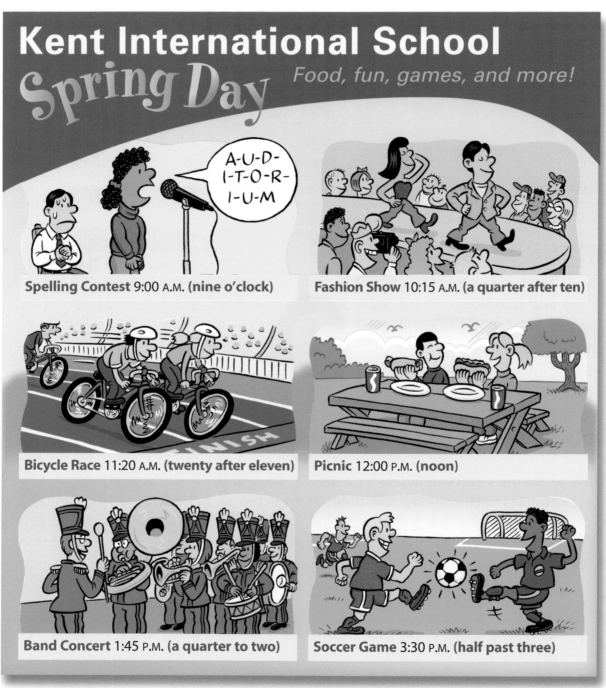

Kent International School
Spring Day — *Food, fun, games, and more!*

A-U-D-I-T-O-R-I-U-M

Spelling Contest 9:00 A.M. (nine o'clock)

Fashion Show 10:15 A.M. (a quarter after ten)

Bicycle Race 11:20 A.M. (twenty after eleven)

Picnic 12:00 P.M. (noon)

Band Concert 1:45 P.M. (a quarter to two)

Soccer Game 3:30 P.M. (half past three)

B What time are the events? Complete the sentences.

1. The _____ is at a quarter after ten.

2. The picnic is at _____ .

3. The soccer game is at _____ .

2. Language focus

A Yoshi and Paulo are at Spring Day. Listen and practice.

Yoshi Are you excited about Spring Day?

Paulo Yes, I am. I'm in the spelling contest and the soccer game.

Yoshi Uh, what time is the spelling contest?

Paulo It's at nine o'clock. What time is it now?

Yoshi It's five minutes after nine.

Paulo Oh, no! I'm already late.

> **What time . . . ?**
>
> **What time** is it now?
> **It's** 9:05. (It's nine-oh-five.)
> **It's** five (minutes) after nine.
>
> **What time** is the spelling contest?
> **It's** at nine (o'clock).

B It's Spring Day at another International School. Write questions and answers. Then listen and check.

1. (bicycle race) _What time is the bicycle race?_
   (10:15) _It's at a quarter after ten._

2. (fashion show) _____
   (3:30) _____

3. (band concert) _____
   (12:20) _____

4. (picnic) _____
   (1:15) _____

5. (soccer game) _____
   (2:45) _____

3. Listening

What time is it now? Listen and check (✓) the correct time.

1. ☑ 10:05   2. ☐ 1:45   3. ☐ 12:15   4. ☐ 3:45   5. ☐ 11:00
   ☐ 10:25   ☐ 1:30   ☐ 12:00   ☐ 3:30   ☐ 10:50

1. Reading

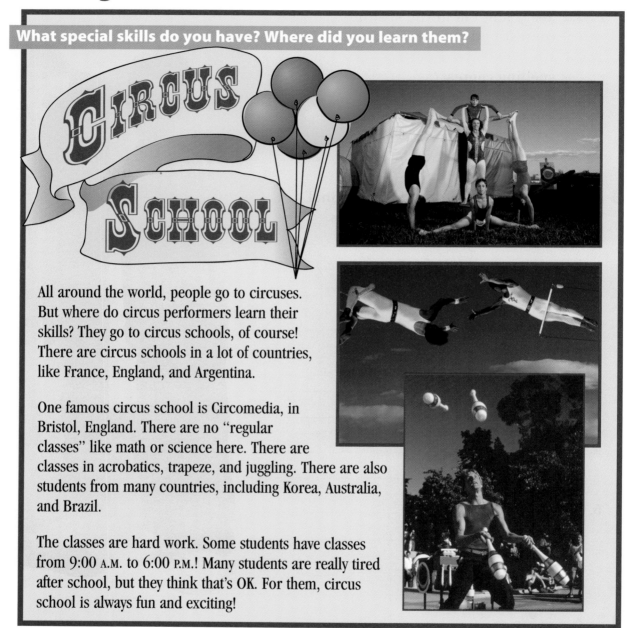

What special skills do you have? Where did you learn them?

CIRCUS SCHOOL

All around the world, people go to circuses. But where do circus performers learn their skills? They go to circus schools, of course! There are circus schools in a lot of countries, like France, England, and Argentina.

One famous circus school is Circomedia, in Bristol, England. There are no "regular classes" like math or science here. There are classes in acrobatics, trapeze, and juggling. There are also students from many countries, including Korea, Australia, and Brazil.

The classes are hard work. Some students have classes from 9:00 A.M. to 6:00 P.M.! Many students are really tired after school, but they think that's OK. For them, circus school is always fun and exciting!

◁)) **A** Read about a circus school.

B Are these sentences true or false? Check (✓) T (true) or F (false).

	T	F
1. There are circus schools in many areas of the world.	✓	☐
2. All the students at Circomedia are from England.	☐	☐
3. Circomedia has classes in science and math.	☐	☐
4. There are classes in the morning at Circomedia.	☐	☐
5. Many students think circus school is boring.	☐	☐

C Compare Circomedia with your school. Write *S* (same) or *D* (different).

Circomedia school	Your school
1. There are classes at 9:00 A.M.	_____
2. There are classes in juggling.	_____
3. There are no classes in math or science.	_____
4. There are students from other countries.	_____
5. Sometimes students are tired after school.	_____
6. There is special circus equipment.	_____
7. Many students think school is fun.	_____

2. Listening

Rachel and Tom talk about their schools. Whose school has these facilities? Listen and check (✓) the correct schools.

	Swimming pool	Tennis courts	Baseball field	Media center	Language lab
Rachel's school	☑	☐	☐	☐	☐
Tom's school	☐	☐	☐	☐	☐

3. Writing

A Complete the web.

Classes and times

_____   _____   _____
_____   _____   _____

(**My school**)

Facilities

_____   _____
_____   _____

Students

Some students . . .
Many students . . .
Sometimes students . . .

B Now write about your school. Use part A and the words in the box to help you.

My school is . . .

. . . class is at . . .
There is / There are . . .

Language chart review

There's / There are	
There's a nice library in my neighborhood.	**There's no** library in my neighborhood.
There are two athletic fields at my school.	**There are no** athletic fields at my school.

Is there a / Are there any . . . ?	
Is there a park in your neighborhood?	**Are there any** restaurants in your neighborhood?
Yes, **there is.**	Yes, **there are.**
No, **there isn't.**	No, **there aren't.**

There's = There is   isn't = is not   aren't = are not

A Complete the e-mails with *there's, there are, there's no,*
and *there are no.*

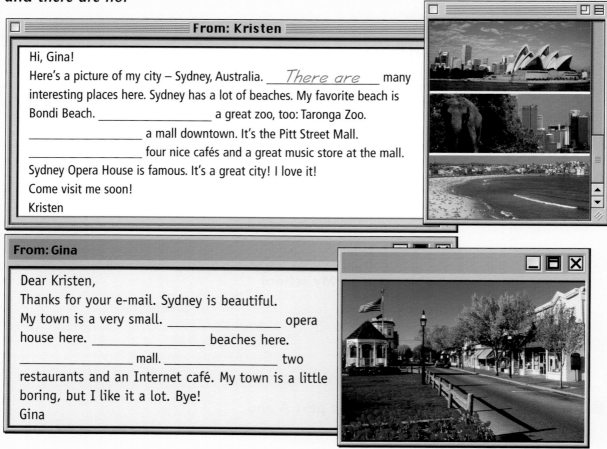

From: Kristen

Hi, Gina!
Here's a picture of my city – Sydney, Australia. _There are_ many
interesting places here. Sydney has a lot of beaches. My favorite beach is
Bondi Beach. _____ a great zoo, too: Taronga Zoo.
_____ a mall downtown. It's the Pitt Street Mall.
_____ four nice cafés and a great music store at the mall.
Sydney Opera House is famous. It's a great city! I love it!
Come visit me soon!
Kristen

From: Gina

Dear Kristen,
Thanks for your e-mail. Sydney is beautiful.
My town is a very small. _____ opera
house here. _____ beaches here.
_____ mall. _____ two
restaurants and an Internet café. My town is a little
boring, but I like it a lot. Bye!
Gina

B Write questions and answers about Gina's town.

1. (a zoo) **Q:** _Is there a zoo?_____ **A:** _No, there isn't._____

2. (a café) **Q:** _____ **A:** _____

3. (any beaches) **Q:** _____ **A:** _____

4. (a mall) **Q:** _____ **A:** _____

C Sandra and Tyler are talking. Unscramble the words to make questions.

Sandra *Is there a volleyball game today?*

> there   a   game   is   volleyball   today

Tyler Yes, there is.

Sandra _____

> is   what   game   the   time

Tyler It's at 10:00.

Sandra _____

> time   what   now   it   is

Tyler It's 9:45.

Language chart review

What time . . . ?	on / at

What time is it?
   It's ten forty-five.
What time is the concert?
   It's at six.
	I have art **on** Tuesday.
	Lunch is **at** 11:15.
	There's a soccer game **on** Monday **at** 5:00.

D Look at the posters, and write sentences.

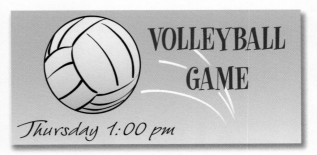

1. *There's a concert on Tuesday at eight o'clock.*

2. _____

3. _____

4. _____

People and countries

1. Vocabulary

◁» **A** English is a major language in at least 75 countries.
Here are some of the countries. Listen and practice.

English Around the World
They speak English in . . .

Belize   England   India

South Africa   Singapore   New Zealand

Source: *The Cambridge Factfinder*, 4th edition

◁» **B** Hannah's parents plan a world vacation. Listen. Number the
countries in the order that the family will visit them.

| ☐ Canada | ☐ India | ☐ Belize | ☐ South Africa |
| ☐ England | ☐ New Zealand | ☐ Singapore | *1* the United States |

2. Language focus

•

A Hannah shows her vacation photos to Mark. Listen and practice.

is / isn't; are / aren't in short answers	
Is she from India?	Yes, she **is**.
Is he from Singapore?	No, he **isn't**.
Are they from Singapore?	Yes, they **are**.
Are they from New Zealand?	No, they **aren't**.
isn't = is not aren't = are not	

Hannah Here I am with Tom and Bruce.

Mark Are they from England?

Hannah No, they aren't. They're from New Zealand.

Mark Wow! Look at this photo. These girls are very pretty! Are they from Singapore?

Hannah Yes, they are. They have e-mail! I can introduce you.

Mark Great! And this boy? Is he from Singapore, too?

Hannah No, he isn't. He's from India. His name is Ravi. And this is his friend, Usha.

Mark Is she from India, too?

Hannah Yes, she is.

Mark Wow! You have a lot of new friends!

Hannah Yes, and they all speak English!

B Look at part A. Answer the questions. Then listen and check.

1. Are Tom and Bruce from Canada? _No, they aren't._

2. Is Ravi from India? _____

3. Is Usha from Singapore? _____

4. Are the girls from England? _____

5. Are the girls from Singapore? _____

3. Speaking

•

Complete the sentences with names of places.
A classmate guesses the places.

_____He's from New Zealand._____

He's from _____ .

She's from _____ .

They're from _____ .

Classmate Is he from Belize?

You No, he isn't.

Classmate Is he from New Zealand?

You Yes, he is.

Nationalities

1. Vocabulary

A Take Yoshi's Internet quiz. Match the photos to the correct texts.
Then listen and practice.

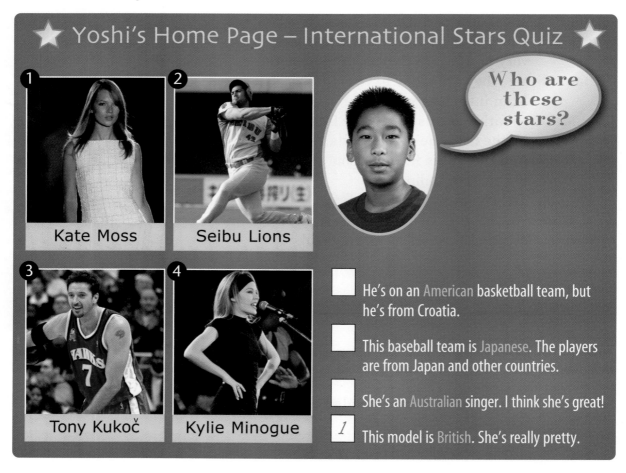

Yoshi's Home Page – International Stars Quiz

Who are these stars?

1 Kate Moss
2 Seibu Lions
3 Tony Kukoč
4 Kylie Minogue

☐ He's on an American basketball team, but he's from Croatia.

☐ This baseball team is Japanese. The players are from Japan and other countries.

☐ She's an Australian singer. I think she's great!

1 This model is British. She's really pretty.

B Complete the chart with the words in the box.
Then listen and practice.

☑ American	☐ Brazilian	☐ Canadian	☐ Japanese	☐ Peruvian	☐ South Korean
☐ Australian	☐ British	☐ French	☐ Mexican	☐ Puerto Rican	☐ Spanish

Place	Nationality	Place	Nationality
1. the United States	*American*	7. South Korea	
2. Japan		8. Australia	
3. Brazil		9. Puerto Rico	
4. Spain		10. Peru	
5. England		11. Mexico	
6. France		12. Canada	

2. Pronunciation Syllable stress

🔊 Listen. Underline the stressed part of each word. Then listen again and practice.

1. Ca <u>na</u> di an
2. <u>Mex</u> i can
3. Ko re an
4. Pe ru vi an

5. Bri tish
6. Jap a nese
7. A mer i can
8. Span ish

9. Puer to Ri can
10. Bra zil ian
11. Aus tral ian
12. Co lom bi an

3. Language focus

🔊 Complete Yoshi's home page with *isn't* or *aren't*. Who are these stars? Listen and check.

isn't / aren't in statements

He **isn't** American.

His movies **aren't** all in English.

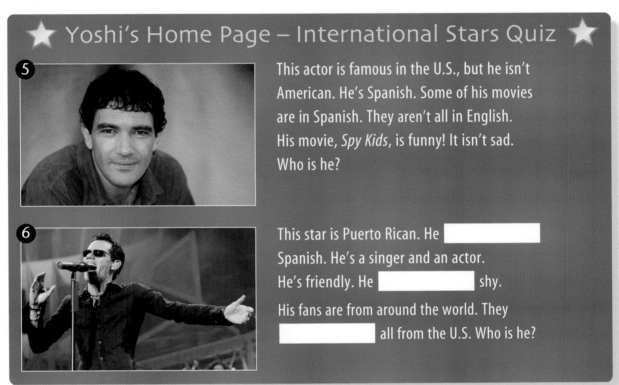

★ Yoshi's Home Page – International Stars Quiz ★

5 This actor is famous in the U.S., but he isn't American. He's Spanish. Some of his movies are in Spanish. They aren't all in English. His movie, *Spy Kids*, is funny! It isn't sad. Who is he?

6 This star is Puerto Rican. He _____ Spanish. He's a singer and an actor. He's friendly. He _____ shy. His fans are from around the world. They _____ all from the U.S. Who is he?

4. Speaking

A Write false statements about stars.

Kate Moss is Peruvian.

B Read your false statements. Your classmates correct them.

Kate Moss is Peruvian.

She isn't Peruvian. She's British.

Mini-review

1. Language check

A Look at Jenny's e-mail address book. Then correct the sentences below.

Full name	City / Place	E-mail addres
Amanda Dart	Sydney, Australia	adart@prest
Mike Maynard	Montreal, Canada	mmaynard@i
Emiko Koga	Kyoto, Japan	koga@iscorl
Jack Crowe	Melbourne, Australia	jackc@prism
Juan Rivera	Acapulco, Mexico	jrivera@yalo
Peter Stockwell	Vancouver, Canada	Pstock3@cox
Claudia Ferreira	São Paulo, Brazil	claferr@spe

1. Emiko is Canadian. *She isn't Canadian. She's Japanese.*

2. Melbourne and Sydney are in Japan. *They . . .*

3. Claudia is from Mexico. _____

4. Juan and Amanda are from Canada. _____

5. Peter is American. _____

6. Kyoto is in Brazil. _____

7. Montreal and Vancouver are in the United States. _____

B Now check your answers with a classmate.

> Is Emiko Canadian?

> No, she isn't. She's Japanese.

2. Listening

🔊 Paulo talks about his e-pals. Listen and check (✓) their nationalities. Then compare with a classmate.

1. Lee	☐ South Korean	☐ Puerto Rican
2. Ashley and Helen	☐ Australian	☐ British
3. Alberto	☐ Peruvian	☐ Mexican
4. Angela and Hector	☐ American	☐ Spanish

> Lee is ....

> That's right.

3. Game Countries Puzzle

A Unscramble the letters to make country names.

uAliasrta	*Australia*	cenarF	_____
alzriB	_____	iladn	_____
aaanCd	_____	xeMoci	_____
ndaEnlg	_____	niaSp	_____

B Write the country names from part A to complete the puzzle.

Lesson 33 Holidays

1. Vocabulary

◁)) **A** Listen and practice the months of the year.

January February March April May June July
August September October November December

◁)) **B** When are these holidays in the U.S.? Complete the sentences with the months below. Then listen and practice.

☐ February ☑ May ☐ July ☐ October ☐ November ☐ December

1
Mother's Day is in ___May___ .

2
Thanksgiving is in _____ .

3
Valentine's Day is in _____ .

4
Halloween is in _____ .

5
Independence Day is in _____ .

6
New Year's Eve is in _____ .

C Play a chain game. Talk about your favorite holiday.

Sarah What's your favorite holiday, Mina?
Mina It's Valentine's Day. It's in February.

→ **Mina** What's your favorite holiday, Robert?
Robert It's Thanksgiving. It's in November.

→ **Robert** What's your . . . ?

2. Language focus

When is . . . ?

When is Independence Day?
It's **in July**.

🔊 **A** Jenny chats with her e-pal, José.
Listen and practice.

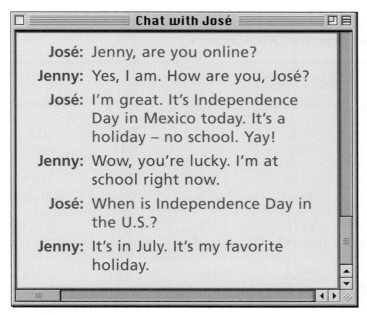

Chat with José

José: Jenny, are you online?

Jenny: Yes, I am. How are you, José?

José: I'm great. It's Independence Day in Mexico today. It's a holiday – no school. Yay!

Jenny: Wow, you're lucky. I'm at school right now.

José: When is Independence Day in the U.S.?

Jenny: It's in July. It's my favorite holiday.

B Look at 1B. Write four questions about holidays in the U.S. Then ask and answer the questions.

When is New Year's Eve?

1. _____

2. _____

3. _____

4. _____

When is New Year's Eve?   It's in December.

3. Listening

🔊 **A** When are these holidays? Listen and match the two parts of each sentence.

1. Independence Day in Mexico is in ____   a. January.
2. Thanksgiving Day in Canada is in ____   b. May.
3. Children's Day in Japan is in ____   c. September.
4. Australia Day is in ____   d. October.

B Ask and answer questions about holidays in your country.

When is Carnaval in Brazil?   It's in February or March.

Around the World 93

34 Important days

1. Vocabulary

🔊 **A** Look at the calendar. Listen and practice the numbers.

March

Sunday	Monday	Tuesday	Wednesday	Thursday	Friday	Saturday
1st first	2nd second	3rd third	4th fourth	5th fifth	6th sixth	7th seventh
8th eighth	9th ninth	10th tenth	11th eleventh	12th twelfth	13th thirteenth	14th fourteenth
15th fifteenth	16th sixteenth	17th seventeenth	18th eighteenth	19th nineteenth	20th twentieth	21st twenty-first
22nd twenty-second	23rd twenty-third	24th twenty-fourth	25th twenty-fifth	26th twenty-sixth	27th twenty-seventh	28th twenty-eighth
29th twenty-ninth	30th thirtieth	31st thirty-first				

🔊 **B** Say these dates. Then listen and practice.

January 1st	April 5th	July 3rd	October 31st
February 22nd	May 17th	August 12th	November 18th
March 13th	June 11th	September 9th	December 24th

2. Listening

🔊 Paulo and Nicole make a list of birthdays.
Listen and complete the chart.

Name	Birthday
Sandra	*September twelfth*
Jenny	
Tyler	
Yoshi	
Nicole	
Paulo	

3. Language focus

🔊 **A** Jeremy and Jane are e-pals. They write about their favorite months. Listen and practice.

Jeremy – Chicago, U.S.

The first day of school is in September. And my best friend's birthday is on September 28th. He has great parties. I'm always happy in September.

My favorite month is December. The last day of school is on December 7th. My birthday is on December 11th. There are a lot of holidays in December, too.

Jane – Auckland, New Zealand

🔊 **B** Complete the sentences with *in* or *on*. For 5 and 6, use your own information. Then listen and check.

1. There are a lot of holidays ___*in*___ November.

2. Valentine's Day is _____ February 14th.

3. Halloween is _____ October 31st.

4. Mother's Day is _____ May.

5. My last day of school is _____ .

6. My best friend's birthday is _____ .

4. Speaking

Play a chain game. Learn about your classmates' birthdays.

Sarah When's your birthday, Robert?
Robert It's on August 21st.

        Robert When's your birthday, Mina?
        Mina It's on January 3rd.

                Mina When's your birthday, . . . ?

1. Reading

How do you say "Hello" in your country? How many ways can you say "Hello"?

Teens Around the World

Ni hau! That's "Hello" in Mandarin Chinese. I'm from Beijing, China. My name is Guo Yi Min. *Guo* is my family name. In China, the family name is first. *Yi Min* means "smart and happy" in Chinese. I like my name a lot!

¡Hola! I'm Carmen. I'm from Cuzco, a town in Peru. *Hola* is "Hello" in Spanish. I speak Spanish and Quechua. Quechua is a native South American language. I speak Quechua with my grandparents. *Allillanchu* is "How are you?" in Quechua.

Assalam Alaikum! My name is Habib. I'm Egyptian. In Egypt, we speak Arabic. *Assalam Alaikum* is a greeting. It's like "Hello." Many English words are from Arabic – words like "candy" and "coffee."

A Read the article about these teens.

B Correct the sentences.

1. Guo Yi Min speaks ~~Japanese.~~ *Guo Yi Min speaks Chinese.*
2. *Hola* means "Good-bye." _____
3. Habib speaks Egyptian. _____
4. Carmen speaks French and Quechua. _____
5. The word "Hello" is Arabic. _____
6. *Yi Min* means "quiet and happy." _____

C Read the article again. Then complete the chart.

	Country	Nationality	Language(s)
Yi Min	_____	_____	_Chinese_
Habib	_Egypt_	_____	_____
Carmen	_____	_Peruvian_	_____

2. Listening

A What language do you hear? Listen and guess.
Write the number next to the language.

☐ Arabic   ☐ German   ☐ Japanese   ☐ Russian

☐ French   ☐ Italian   ☐ Korean   ☐ Spanish

B Now listen and check your answers.

3. Writing

A Complete the information about yourself.

"Hello" (in my language): _____   My country: _____

My name: _____   My language(s): _____

My nationality: _____   My birthday: _____

My city: _____   My favorite holiday: _____

B Use part A to write an article about yourself.

"Hello" in my language is . . .

Review

Language chart review

isn't / aren't in statements	*isn't / aren't* in short answers	Questions with *when in / on*
She **isn't** American.	**Is she** American?	**When is** Bobby's birthday?
They **aren't** French.	Yes, **she is**.	It's **in** June.
	No, **she isn't**.	It's **on** June 2nd.
	Are they Peruvian?	
	Yes, **they are**.	
	No, **they aren't**.	

A Read the article. Then answer the questions.

Six Young Stars

Shakira – singer
Country: Colombia
Birthday: February 2, 1977
First CD at 13

Daniel Radcliffe – actor
Country: England
Birthday: July 23, 1989
Star of *Harry Potter* movies at 12

Mary-Kate and Ashley Olsen – singers and actors
Country: the United States
Birthday: June 13, 1986
First video at 7

Gustavo Kuerten – tennis player
Country: Brazil
Birthday: September 10, 1976
Professional player at 19

Zhang Ziyi – actor
Country: China
Birthday: February 9, 1980
International star at 20

1. Is Shakira from Brazil? *No, she isn't.* _____

2. Is Gustavo Kuerten a soccer player? _____

3. Are Mary-Kate and Ashley Olsen models? _____

4. Is Zhang Ziyi Chinese? _____

5. Are Daniel Radcliffe and Zhang Ziyi actors? _____

6. Is Gustavo's birthday in June? _____

B Look at part A. Write about two people.

Shakira is a singer. She's Colombian.

Her birthday is on February 2nd.

1. _____

_____

2. _____

_____

C Look at Lisa's calendar. Write a question for each answer.

October	
22 Monday *Kate's birthday*	**25** Thursday *the Shakira concert!*
23 Tuesday	**26** Friday *the Halloween dance*
24 Wednesday United Nations Day	**27** *Movie night* Saturday **28** *the soccer game* Sunday

October/November	
29 Monday	**1** Thursday
30 Tuesday	**2** Friday *Josh's birthday*
31 Wednesday *BOO!* Halloween	**3** Saturday **4** Sunday

1. **Q:** *When is the Halloween dance?*   **A:** It's on October 26th.
2. **Q:** _____ **A:** It's on October 27th.
3. **Q:** _____ **A:** It's on November 2nd.
4. **Q:** _____ **A:** It's on October 25th.

D Look at Lisa's calendar again. Correct the sentences with *isn't* and *aren't*. Spell out the numbers.

1. Josh's birthday is on November first. *Josh's birthday isn't on*

November first. It's on November second.

2. Halloween and United Nations Day are in November. _____

_____

3. Movie night is on October twenty-eighth. _____

_____

4. The soccer game is on October thirty-first. _____

_____

5. Kate's birthday is in November. _____

Favorite places

1. Vocabulary

🔊 **A** These are three students' favorite places. Match the photos to the correct texts. Then listen and practice.

1 beach

2 zoo

3 wax museum

☐ This place is in San Diego. It's interesting. It's not boring. There are animals from around the world. There are pandas from China.

☐ This place is in New York. It's fun, but it's always crowded. There are wax models of famous singers and actors. There is even a model of Harry Potter.

☐ This place is in Puerto Rico. It's beautiful. It's really exciting, too. It's my favorite place for a vacation.

B Read the words. What places do you think of? Complete the chart and then tell your classmates.

Word	Place		Word	Place
beautiful	*Ipanema Beach*		interesting	_____
boring	_____		crowded	_____
exciting	_____		fun	_____

> Ipanema Beach is beautiful.

2. Language focus

What's it like?

What's it like?
It's fun.

A Tyler and Yoshi talk about their favorite places. Listen and practice.

Tyler What's your favorite place in Tokyo, Yoshi?

Yoshi It's Odaiba.

Tyler What's it like?

Yoshi It's fun. There are a lot of things there. There are beaches, parks, stores, and museums. Joypolis Park is also there.

Tyler What's it like?

Yoshi It's great. It has a lot of video games.

B Complete the conversation. Listen and check. Then practice.

Tyler I like New York a lot.

Yoshi _____

Tyler It's big and exciting. I like the Empire State Building, too.

Yoshi _____

Tyler It's really beautiful. And there's an observatory on the 102nd floor.

C Ask a classmate about a favorite place in your town or city.

A What's your favorite place in . . . ?

B It's . . .

A What's it like?

B It's . . .

3. Listening

Jenny, Paulo, and Sandra talk to Tyler about a museum. What's it like? Listen and check (✓) the correct words.

	beautiful	interesting	exciting	fun	crowded	boring
Jenny	✓		✓			
Paulo						
Sandra						

37 Talent show

1. Vocabulary ●

🔊 **A** There is a talent show at Kent International School. Look at the bulletin board. Label the photos with the words in the box. Then listen and practice.

> ☐ dance ☑ play Ping-Pong ☐ sing
> ☐ draw ☐ play the guitar ☐ skateboard

Enter the Talent Show!

1. play Ping-Pong
2.
3.
4.
5.
6.

B Who in your class can enter the talent show? Write one name for each category.

Category	Name	Category	Name
dance	_____	sing	_____
play the guitar	_____	play Ping-Pong	_____
draw	_____	skateboard	_____

2. Language focus

A Paulo and Sandra talk about the talent show. Listen and practice.

Paulo	Look! There's a talent show on Sunday. Let's enter.
Sandra	Um . . . no, thanks.
Paulo	Oh, come on. I can play the guitar. I can't sing. Can you sing?
Sandra	No, I can't. I can't sing at all.
Paulo	Can you dance?
Sandra	Yes, I can. But . . .
Paulo	So, let's enter the show.
Sandra	You and me? You're kidding! I'm too shy.

can / can't	
I **can** dance.	She **can't** sing.
Can you dance?	**Can** she sing?
Yes, I **can.**	**No,** she **can't.**
Use *can* for all subjects: *I, you, he, she, we, they*	

B Write two things Paulo and Sandra can and can't do. Then listen and check.

1. Paulo _____.
2. Paulo _____.
3. Sandra _____.
4. Sandra _____.

3. Speaking

Read the survey. Write questions 4 and 5. Complete the survey for yourself. Then ask a classmate the questions.

What can you do?	You		Your classmate	
	Yes	No	Yes	No
1. Can you skateboard?	☐	☐	☐	☐
2. Can you draw?	☐	☐	☐	☐
3. Can you play Ping-Pong?	☐	☐	☐	☐
4. _____	☐	☐	☐	☐
5. _____	☐	☐	☐	☐

Can you skateboard?

Yes, I can.

No, I can't.

4. Pronunciation *can* and *can't*

A Listen to the pronunciation of *can* and *can't*.

He **can** sing.   He **can't** dance.

B Listen and check (✓) *can* or *can't*. Then listen again and practice.

1. ☐ can
   ☐ can't
2. ☐ can
   ☐ can't
3. ☐ can
   ☐ can't
4. ☐ can
   ☐ can't
5. ☐ can
   ☐ can't

Mini-review

1. Language check

A Write a question and answer for each picture.

1. _Can she sing?_
   No, she can't.

2. _____
   _____

3. _____
   _____

4. _____
   _____

B Match the questions to the answers.

1. What's your home like? _b_
2. Can you swim? _____
3. What's your best friend like? _____
4. Is your English class interesting? _____
5. What's your country like? _____
6. Can your teacher play soccer? _____

a. She's fun and really friendly.
b. It's nice. It has four bedrooms.
c. Yes, I can. It's really fun!
d. Yes, it is. And my teacher is nice, too.
e. No, she can't. But she can play tennis.
f. It's beautiful. But some places are crowded.

C Now ask and answer the questions in part B. Give your own information.

What's your home like?

It's . . .

2. Game Can You . . . ?

Play the game with a classmate. Use things in your bag as game markers.

To begin:

- Close your eyes and touch one of the numbers.
- Move your game marker that number of spaces.
- Read the question. Can you do what it says?
  - ▶ Yes. Follow the green arrow and move ahead.
  - ▶ No. Follow the red arrow and move back.
- On a "free space," ask a classmate any question. On your next turn, touch one of the numbers and move that number of spaces.

Lesson 38 School fashion

1. Vocabulary

🔊 **A** These three students want new school uniforms. Listen and write their names under the correct pictures.

☐ Sergio ☐ Mei Lin ☐ Matt

blouse
sweater
skirt
shoes

shirt
tie
jacket
pants

T-shirt
shorts
socks
sneakers

_____ _____ _____

🔊 **B** Listen and practice.

🔊 **C** Look at the colors. Listen and practice.

1 blue   **2** white   **3** green   **4** pink   **5** orange

6 red   **7** black   **8** brown   **9** yellow   **10** purple

D Look at part A. Complete the descriptions of the school uniforms.

> **adjective + noun**
>
> white blouse
> black shoes

1. Mei Lin's school uniform is a _pink_ blouse, a blue _skirt_ , _black_ shoes, and a blue _sweater_ .

2. Matt's school uniform is a _____ shirt, a green _____ , a _____ tie, and _____ pants.

3. Sergio's school uniform is a _____ T-shirt, _____ shorts, yellow _____ , and _____ sneakers.

2. Language focus

A Andrew and Luke talk about their new school uniform. Listen and practice.

> **What color is / are . . . ?**
>
> **What color is** the shirt?
> **It's** white.
>
> **What color are** the pants?
> **They're** blue.

Andrew Oh, wow! There's a new school uniform for next year.

Luke Really? What's it like?

Andrew It's OK. There's a shirt, a jacket, and pants.

Luke What color is the shirt?

Andrew It's white.

Luke That's nice. What color are the pants?

Andrew They're blue.

Luke And what color is the jacket?

Andrew It's purple.

Luke Purple? Oh, no!

Andrew Luke, I'm kidding. The jacket is blue, too.

B What is your dream uniform like? Complete the questions with *is* or *are*. Then answer the questions. Tell your classmates.

1. What color ____*is*____ the shirt? *It's orange.* _____

2. What color _____ the pants? _____

3. What color _____ the socks? _____

4. What color _____ the sweater? _____

5. What color _____ the shoes? _____

> The shirt is orange. The pants are . . .

3. Listening

Four students talk on the radio about school fashion. Listen and number the pictures.

39 Teen tastes

1. Vocabulary

🔊 **A** Read about students' favorite things. Match the photos to the correct sentences. Then listen and practice.

- ☐ My favorite music is rap.
- ☐ My favorite school subject is biology.
- ☑ My favorite food is pizza.
- ☐ My favorite food is hot dogs.
- ☐ My favorite music is rock.
- ☐ My favorite music is classical.
- ☐ My favorite school subject is Italian.
- ☐ My favorite food is hamburgers.

1
2
3
4

5
6
7
8

B Complete these statements. Then tell your classmates.

My favorite music is _____ .

My favorite school subject is _____ .

My favorite food is _____ .

> My favorite music is . . .

2. Language focus

love / like / don't like

I **love** rock music.
I **like** rap music.
I **don't like** classical music.

🔊 **A** **What do Yoshi and Jenny like?**
Listen and practice.

I'm a big music fan. I love rock music, and I like rap music. I can play the electric guitar. I don't like classical music. I think it's boring. My friends and I have a rock band. It's really cool.

Yoshi

I love school! I really like all of my classes, and I like my teachers and my friends. The food in the cafeteria is great. There are hot dogs and hamburgers. There's one thing I don't like about school – the homework!

Jenny

B **What about you? Complete the statements with** *love, like,* **or**
don't like. **Then compare with a classmate.**

1. I _____ rap music.
2. I _____ math.
3. I _____ soccer.
4. I _____ pizza.
5. I _____ English.
6. I _____ the beach.

7. I _____ the first day of school.
8. I _____ classical music.
9. I _____ hot dogs.
10. I _____ my first name.
11. I _____ my city / town.
12. I _____ my school.

I love rap music. I think it's cool.

I don't like rap music. I think it's boring.

3. Listening

🔊 **Nicole talks about her favorite things. Listen and check (✓) the**
correct things.

Sport	Music	School subject	Food	Clothing
✓ volleyball	☐ rap	☐ art	☐ hamburgers	☐ jacket
☐ tennis	☐ rock	☐ science	☐ pizza	☐ sneakers

Connections

1. Reading

What are your favorite school events? When are they?

Kent International School
Student Yearbook
HIGHLIGHTS OF THE YEAR

Here are some of our favorite events.

"It's always very crowded, but I really like the party! October 31st is an exciting day for everyone. There are interesting costumes! What a great day!"
— *Ms. Davis, science teacher*

Halloween Party

"I love this event at Mason Beach. I can play volleyball, and I can swim. There are a lot of other sports, too. There are some great shops, and the beach is really fun. We all eat a lot."
— *Tyler Foster*

Class Picnic

"What's my favorite event like? It's really cool. Look at Jenny's hair. She loves green. I think she looks great. And look at my hair. Pink and orange are my favorite colors. And we can wear crazy clothes, too. It's fun — I just love it!"
— *Sandra García*

Crazy Day

A Read about the events.

B What school events are the students talking about?
Write the letter of the event.

a. Crazy Day   b. Class Picnic   c. Halloween Party

1. "Look at Mr. Diaz's weird hair and those purple and green shorts." _a_
2. "My favorite school event is in October." ____
3. "I play basketball at my favorite event." ____
4. "There are a lot of weird costumes." ____
5. "My best friend can swim well, so she really loves it." ____
6. "Ms. Clark's hair is black and red. Those are our school colors." ____

2. Listening

🔊 Students talk about these events and holidays. What do they say
about them? Listen and check (✓) the correct words.

	exciting	boring	interesting	fun
Thanksgiving	☐	☐	☐	☐
School Spring Day	☐	☐	☐	☐
New Year's Eve	☐	☐	☐	☐

3. Writing

A Complete the chart. Write one holiday, place, and event you like
and one you don't like. Then write the reasons.

	Like	Why	Don't like	Why
Holiday				
Place				
Event				

B Use part A to write about yourself.

Holiday: _I like . . .   It's . . ._

_____

I don't like . . .   It's . . .

Place: _____

_____

_____

Event: _____

_____

_____

Language chart review

What's . . . like?	love / like / don't like	can / can't

What's New York **like?**
 It's fun.
	I love this town.
	 I like the mall.
	 I don't like my room.
		I can sing.
		 He **can't** sing.
		 Can you sing?
		     Yes, I can. / No, I can't.
		 Can they play soccer?
		     Yes, they **can. / No,** they **can't.**

What color is / are . . . ?		
What color is Kate's sweater? **It's** blue. **What color are** Kate's shoes? **They're** black.		can't = cannot

A Mary meets Alex. Complete the conversation with the sentences
in the box. Write the letters in the boxes.

☐ a. I can play the guitar. I'm pretty good.
☐ b. Well, I love soccer, but there are no soccer fields near here.
☑ c. Yes, I am. I'm Alex.
☐ d. No, I can't. I don't like baseball. Can you play?
☐ e. It's great! The people are friendly, and there are a lot of beautiful places.
☐ f. Yeah, it's interesting. But this town is boring.

Mary   Excuse me. Are you Tim's cousin from Mexico?
Alex   ☐ c
Mary   Hi, I'm Mary. So, what's Mexico like?
Alex   ☐
Mary   Wow, that's cool! Do you like the U.S.?
Alex   ☐
Mary   Really? Why is it boring? I love our town.
Alex   ☐
Mary   Yeah, you're right. But there's a baseball field. Can you play baseball?
Alex   ☐
Mary   Yes, I can. I love baseball. So, what other things can you do?
Alex   ☐
Mary   Really? I like the guitar, too.

B What do you think Alex and Mary say?
Circle the correct words.

Alex

1. I (like / don't like) the U.S.

2. I (like / don't like) this town.

3. I (can / can't) play baseball.

Mary

4. I (can / can't) play baseball.

5. I (like / don't like) this town.

6. I (like / don't like) music.

C Look at the picture on page 112. What are Mary's clothes like? What are Alex's clothes like? Check (✓) the false sentences.

☑ 1. Alex's pants are brown. ☐ 5. Mary's shoes are green.
☐ 2. Mary's T-shirt is red. ☐ 6. Alex's sneakers are purple.
☐ 3. Alex's shirt is white. ☐ 7. Mary's hat is blue.
☐ 4. Mary's skirt is blue. ☐ 8. Alex's jacket is black.

D Now correct the false sentences in part C.

1. _Alex's pants are black._
2. _____
3. _____
4. _____

E Write the questions or the answers about Kate.

1. **Q:** _What color is Kate's blouse?_

   A: It's white.

2. **Q:** What color are Kate's pants?

   A: _____

3. **Q:** _____

   A: It's green.

4. **Q:** What color is Kate's sweater?

   A: _____

5. **Q:** _____

   A: They're pink.

6. **Q:** What color is Kate's hat?

   A: _____

F Write questions beginning with *Can you*. Then answer the questions with your own information.

1. (sing)   **Q:** _Can you sing?_

   A: _____

2. (skateboard)   **Q:** _____

   A: _____

3. (draw people)   **Q:** _____

   A: _____

4. (play tennis)   **Q:** _____

   A: _____

Theme Project: Make a poster about a classmate.
Themes: Relationships; citizenship
Goal: To create stronger relationships within your classroom community

Prepare

⌂ Complete the chart.

⌂ **Where is your family originally from?**
Find pictures of people and places in
that country. Look in magazines.

⌂ Choose a photo of yourself.
Bring it to class with the pictures.

What's your first name? _____

What's your last name? _____

What country is your family originally from?

_____

Create

👥 Complete the chart for a classmate.
Ask the questions.

ℹ Make a poster of your classmate
on a piece of paper. Use the sample
poster as a model.

What's your first name? _____

What's your last name? _____

What country is your family originally from?

_____

Present

👪 Introduce your classmate
to your group.

This is Anita Pombo. Her family
is originally from Spain.

Hi, Anita!

🔲 Display the posters on the
board. Walk around and
look at all the posters.

Anita Pombo, Spain

Sample poster

UNIT 2

Theme Project: Make a poster about a person who works at your school.
Theme: Citizenship
Goal: To become better acquainted with people in your community

Prepare

Talk to a school worker. Complete the chart. Draw or tape a picture of the worker on a piece of paper.

First name: _____

Last name: _____

City of origin: _____

_____

Job: _____

Create

Make a poster of the school worker on a piece of paper. Use the sample poster as a model.

Present

Introduce the school worker to another group.

> This is Andre Chaves. He's from São Paulo. He's a janitor.

Display the posters on the board. Walk around and look at all the posters.

Name: _Andre Chaves_

From: _São Paulo, Brazil_

Job: _Janitor_

Sample poster

Theme Project: Make a poster for a department store.
Theme: Consumer awareness
Goal: To become aware of the powerful influence of advertising

Prepare

Look in newspapers and magazines. Find advertisements for three things you want. Bring them to class.

Create

Look at all the advertisements. Choose the best advertisements for five things, one for each.

Choose a name for your department store. Make a poster with the advertisements you chose. Use the sample poster as a model.

Present

Show your poster to another group.

> This is Bruno's Department Store. These are T-shirts. This is a TV. That's a . . .

Display the posters on the board. Vote on the most attractive one.

Bruno's Department Store

T-shirts

bag

camera

jeans

T.V.

Sample poster

Theme Project: Make a guide of useful places in your town or city for visitors.
Theme: Citizenship
Goals: To increase your knowledge of your city or town; to provide useful information for visitors

Prepare

What places in your city or town should a visitor know about?
Choose two. Complete the chart.

Name: _____   Name: _____

Address: _____   Address: _____

Telephone number: _____   Telephone number: _____

Create

Look at all the places.
Choose the best two places.

Make a page for a guide
on a piece of paper.
Use the sample page
as a model.

Present

Show your places to
another group.

This is Cha-Chi's Restaurant. It's on
Main Street. Have a sandwich here.

Make a guide. Staple together
all the pages. Make a cover.
Display the book in the
classroom.

Cha-Chi's Restaurant
100 Main Street
555-7890

Have a sandwich!

PAN-AMERICAN BOOKSTORE

25 Lincoln Street
555-1234

Buy a book!

Sample page

Theme Project: Make a group photo album.
Themes: Relationships; multiculturalism
Goal: To create stronger relationships within your classroom community

Prepare

 Who is your favorite relative? Bring a photo of him or her to class.

Create

Make a photo album page of your relative on a piece of paper.
Use the sample album page as a model.

Introduce your relative to the group.

> This is my cousin, Ricardo. He's fifteen.
> He's tall and thin. I think he's
> handsome. He's really cool, too.
> His mother is from Mexico.

Make a group photo album.
Staple together all the pages.
Make a cover.

Present

Show your group photo
album to another group.
Tell them about the
people in the album.

Display the photo albums
in the classroom. Walk around
and look at all of them.

Ricardo
Cousin, 15

Sample album page